Terrance Ta...
A Pocket Guide to East Africa's Uganda & Rwanda

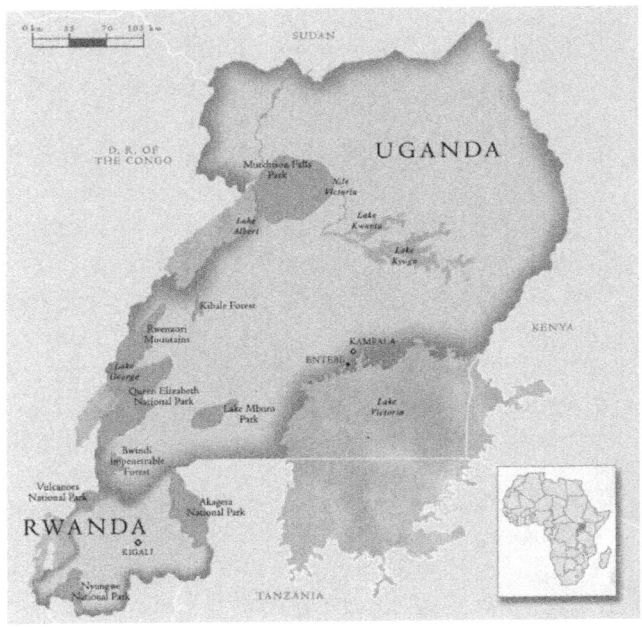

Terrance Zepke

TERRANCE TALKS TRAVEL: A
POCKET GUIDE TO EAST AFRICA'S
UGANDA & RWANDA

Copyright © 2018 by Terrance Zepke

All rights reserved. No part of this book shall be reproduced or transmitted in any form or by any means, electronic, mechanical, magnetic, and photographic including photocopying, recording or by any information storage and retrieval system, without prior written permission of the publisher. No patent liability is assumed with respect to the use of the information contained herein. Although every precaution has been taken in the preparation of this book, the publisher and author assume no responsibility for errors or omissions. Neither is any liability assumed for damages resulting from the use of the information contained herein.

All queries should be directed to: www.safaripublishing.net

To learn more about the author and her books visit www.terrancetalkstravel.com

Library of Congress Cataloging-in-Publication Data

Zepke, Terrance

TERRANCE ZEPKE

Terrance Talks Travel: A Pocket Guide to East Africa's Uganda & Rwanda

America/Terrance Zepke p. cm.

ISBN: 978-1-942738-37-4

1. Travel-East Africa. 2. Adventure Travel-East Africa. 3. Safari-Uganda. 4. Safari-Rwanda. 5. Bwindi Impenetrable Forest. 6. Africa. 7. Volcanoes National Park. 8. East Africa Guidebook. 9. African Wildlife-Mountain Gorillas. 10. Kigali. 11. Kampala. 12. Queen Elizabeth National Park. 13. Murchinson Falls. 14. Entebbe. 15. Virunga Mountains. 16. Gorilla Tracking. I. Title.

First edition

10 9 8 7 6 5 4 3 2 1

Safari Publishing

TERRANCE TALKS TRAVEL: A
POCKET GUIDE TO EAST AFRICA'S
UGANDA & RWANDA

CONTENTS

Introduction, 6
Fast Facts, 12
Gorilla Facts, 25
Gorilla Safaris, 33
About Rwanda, 53
About Uganda, 68
Uganda Safari Parks, 83
Uganda Attractions, 86
Rwanda Attractions, 100
How to Speak Like a Local, 106
Important Information, 108
What to Pack, 121
Resources, 129
Special Dates and Events, 135
Fun Quiz, 141
A Picture Is Worth A Thousand Words, 147
Sneak Peak, *African Safaris,* 180
Titles by Terrance, 199
Index, 224

TERRANCE ZEPKE

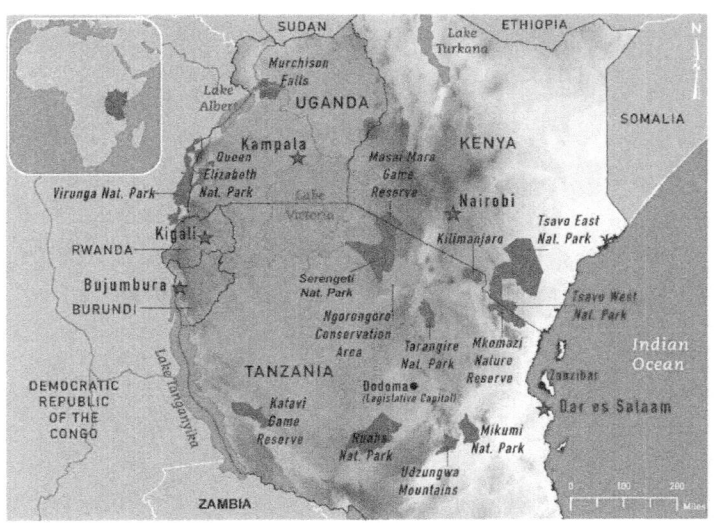

Map of East Africa

Introduction

I have visited Africa many times. I have explored nearly a dozen African countries and enjoyed lots of exciting activities.

I love this continent, which is comprised of fifty-four countries including Uganda and Rwanda. I have lived and traveled all over the world, but always look forward to my visits to this extraordinary place with great anticipation.

Even though I have had the privilege of visiting Africa many times, I am constantly amazed by its people, landscape, and wildlife. I have lived in many extraordinary places, such as London (England), Hilton

Head Island (South Carolina), and Oahu (Hawaii). Additionally, I have traveled to many exotic places, including the Arctic Circle, the Amazon, and Antarctica.

But Africa holds a special place in my heart. It is a new and phenomenal experience every time, especially when I go to more remote regions, such as Uganda and Rwanda. These East African countries offer some of the best safari parks in all of Africa, rare encounters with endangered mountain gorillas, unique lodges, animals you won't see anywhere else (like mountain gorillas and tree-climbing lions), hot air balloon safaris, and much more.

Uganda is small compared to the U.S.—the U.S. is 41 times bigger.

Uganda is the size of Oregon and Rwanda is roughly the size of Maryland.

Rwanda is known as the "Land of a Thousand Hills" while Uganda is known as the "Pearl of Africa." The people, the wildlife, and the parks found in these two extraordinary places make the journey worthwhile.

There is nowhere else in the world, where you can safely see mountain gorillas. If you have seen a gorilla in a zoo, it was probably a lowland gorilla. The reason you won't find mountain gorillas in zoos is that they cannot survive in captivity.

But you will find much more than gorillas in these East African countries. There are hundreds of species of birds and butterflies, thirteen primate species, and many mammals, such as hippos, forest elephants, rare giant forest hogs, leopards, crocodiles, forest buffalos, and tree-climbing lions.

Additionally, there are dozens of safari options, such as foot safaris, boat safaris, hot air balloon safaris, and classic (jeep) safaris. A few places offer night safaris.

But Rwanda and Uganda have even more to offer. Uganda has won "Best Tourist Country." The people are so warm and friendly. The food is better than you might imagine (including complimentary nibbles with your evening sundowner) and the camps are way better than you might imagine. We received complimentary massages after our gorilla trek! Laundry service is included and they even cleaned our boots after our trek. When housekeeping returned them to us, we joked that they were cleaner than when we started.

You can also participate in bungee jumping, bicycle tours, jet boat rides, horseback riding, river surfing, whitewater rafting, quad biking, and more.

Kampala is the capital of Uganda. It is full of restaurants, bars, and nightclubs. Nearby is Lake Victoria and rafting on the Nile or family float trips.

Rwanda's capital is Kigali. Just

like in Kampala, there are many restaurants, nightclubs, and shops.

But once you leave these cities and venture deeper into the African bush, the real adventure begins within their parks, especially Queen Elizabeth National Park, Murchison Falls National Park, and Volcanoes National Park.

Plus, discover hidden gems, such as the Congo Nile Trail, and the Ssese Islands. I discuss all the parks and what they have to offer, so be sure to read this chapter carefully before booking any trip.

So now it's time to turn the page to read, learn, and plan the ultimate adventure –a trip to Rwanda or Uganda—or both!

TERRANCE ZEPKE

Map of Uganda & Rwanda and bordering countries

Fast Facts

SIZE: The country of **Uganda** is 93,065 square miles (241,039 km²). That is the size of the U.S. state of Oregon. Uganda is divided into 111 districts and one city (the capital city of Kampala), which are grouped into four administrative regions: Eastern, Western, Central, and Northern. However, the government is in the process of dividing the districts differently to better allocate government resources.

The country of **Rwanda** is 10,169 square miles (26,338 km²), which is the size of Maryland. The five provinces of Rwanda are divided into thirty districts. Each district is divided into sectors, which are divided into cells, which are divided into villages.

POPULATION: The population of **Uganda** is 41,846,666, and the population of **Rwanda** is 12,033,749.

LANGUAGE: The principal language of **Rwanda** is Kinyarwanda, which is spoken by most Rwandans. The government is now requiring all students to learn English. Also, Swahili and French are widely spoken.

In **Uganda**, the official languages are English and Swahili.

CURRENCY: It is the Ugandan Shilling and the Rwandan Franc. For currency conversion, go to www.oanda.com

TO GET THERE: All flights to **Uganda** will arrive at Entebbe International Airport. There are no direct flights from the U.S. There are direct flights from Doha and some European cities, such as London, Amsterdam, and Istanbul.

National flag of Rwanda

All flights to **Rwanda** will arrive at Gregoire Kayibanda Airport, which is ten miles east of the capital Kigali. There are no direct flights from the

U.S. or Europe at the time of publication.

BEST TIME TO VISIT: For Uganda:

Best Time/High Season: June - August and December to February are the two dry seasons, so these are good times to visit all parks and for gorilla tracking.

Worst Time/Low Season March-May and October - November are the two wet seasons. On the plus side, everything is lush and green and you will see lots of baby animals. Also, the parks are not as crowded. On the bad side, it may rain a lot, and road conditions can be poor, as well as muddy trails that make for difficult trekking.

National flag of Uganda

BEST TIME TO VISIT: For Rwanda:

Best Time/High Season: mid-May – mid-October and December – February are the two dry seasons. Animal sightings are more abundant. As always, the price is higher for travel in the high season.

Worst Time/Low Season: March – mid-May and late October – November. These are the two rainy seasons for Rwanda. The rains can be hard and long or just short downpours that soon give way to clear skies. Generally speaking, it is not a good time for gorilla tracking. However, flora and fauna are beautiful, and it is a great time for bird-watching.

AVERAGE TEMPERATURES

Uganda is sunny most of the year with temperatures rarely rising above 29 degrees Celsius (84 degrees Fahrenheit). The average annual temperature is about 26 degrees Celsius (78° Fahrenheit). January is the sunniest month and April is the least sunny month. Places closer to the Equator, such as Lake Victoria and Kampala have higher temperatures than the mountainous areas, such as Bwindi Impenetrable Forest.

The average temperature for **Rwanda** is 20.5 degrees Celsius (68.9 degrees Fahrenheit). The warmest month is August with an average temperature of 21.5 degrees Celsius (70.7 degrees Fahrenheit). April is the coldest month, having an average temperature of 20 degrees Celsius (68 degrees Fahrenheit).

Check out www.weather.com to find up-to-date weather information for anywhere in Uganda or Rwanda.

FYI: Uganda is about seventy miles north of the equator while Rwanda is about seventy miles south of the equator. This puts Uganda in the Northern Hemisphere and Rwanda in the Southern Hemisphere.

Seasons of Uganda & Rwanda...

SPRING: October-November

SUMMER: December-February

FALL: March-April

WINTER: May-September

BUDGET: This depends on what you're doing. International airfare varies according to your country of origin and time of travel. In low season you can find airfare for less than $1,000, but in high season expect to pay closer to $2,000, on average. Or you can use frequent flier miles and go for free. Your flight may be included in the trip cost if you use a tour operator.

Also, the cost varies greatly depending on whether you choose Rwanda or Uganda. It is $700 for one gorilla tracking permit in Uganda, and it is $1,500 for one gorilla tracking permit in Rwanda. There is also a permit fee for chimpanzee tracking if you choose to do that. Furthermore, the cost depends on what else you choose to do while here and how long you stay. This will be discussed in greater detail later in this reference.

 **UNIQUE EXPERIENCES**: While the highlight is a gorilla safari in Rwanda or Uganda, there are lots of other cool things to do. These include waterfall cruises at Murchison Falls (Uganda), a visit to the Ngamba Chimp Sanctuary (Uganda), a tour of Lubiri Palace (Uganda), explore the Uganda Wildlife Conservation Education Center (Uganda), take a self-guided tour of the Entebbe Botanical Gardens (Uganda), a visit to Dian Fossey's grave (Rwanda), hike Mt. Bisoke (an extinct volcano in Rwanda), bike the Congo Nile Trail (Rwanda), camp at Lake Ruhundo (Rwanda), take a heli-

tour (Rwanda), watch Intore dancers (Rwanda), or kayak Lake Kivu. And you can cap off your experience with a spa treatment at the five-star Sanctuary Gorilla Forest Camp Spa (Uganda) or Iwacu Wellness Center (Rwanda).

The African Leopard is the National Animal of Rwanda.

The Grey-crowned Crane is the National Animal of Uganda.

Best Things About Rwanda & Uganda:

*The parks and safari camps
*Gorilla Tracking
* Wildlife and Nature
*Adventure
*Culture (The people, especially the children, are so friendly!)

*   *   *

FYI: Gorillas are the largest primate in the world.

Gorilla Facts

There are two species of gorillas: the mountain gorilla and the lowland gorilla. The mountain gorilla is found in eastern Africa (Uganda and Rwanda and there are a few in the Democratic Republic of the Congo), while the lowland gorilla makes it home in the forests of central and western Africa (Cameroon, Central African Republic, Congo, Equatorial Guinea, Gabon, Angola, and the Democratic Republic of Congo). Note: The Congo region is divided into two nations -- the Democratic Republic of the Congo (formerly known as Zaire), and the Republic of the Congo, known simply as The Congo.

Besides their habitats being quite different, the differences between mountain gorillas and lowland gorillas are minimal. The hair on a lowland gorilla is shorter and softer. The longer, coarser hair on a mountain gorilla is meant to keep him warm in the cold mountain climate. Both species are about the same height, but mountain gorillas weigh 100-200 pounds more.

Mountain gorilla groups (known as troops) tend to stay in a territory that varies from a few miles to up to sixteen miles (41km). These territories are in national parks located in Uganda and Rwanda, but some cross the border into the Congo.

These places are ideal food sources for gorillas, which are herbivores. This means gorillas don't eat meat as carnivores do, but they have been known to eat small animals.

Typical diet:

*roots and stems
*bamboo shoots
*fruit
*tree bark and pulp
*wild celery
*flowers and leaves
*insects (termites, snails, caterpillars, grubs & ants)

FYI: A male gorilla can consume 40 lbs. of food a day!

Gorilla troops vary from 2-50 gorillas, but two or three dozen per troop is more common. Each troop has a leader, which is always a dominant male silverback. Additionally, there are several younger males, juvenile and adult females, and infants.

As you would imagine, the alpha male makes all the decisions for the troop. He chooses the feeding spots, keeps order, and mandates all group activities. They also father most of the gorillas in the troop. While most silverbacks are not aggressive, they can be if they feel threatened, such as having to defend their troop from a hostile takeover by another silverback or from a poacher.

Female gorillas typically weigh half what a male gorilla weighs.

Gorillas can live 35 years or more in the wild.

Gorillas are creatures of habit. During the day they like to nap, groom, or play. They eat in the mornings and early evenings. Later in the evening, they go to sleep on homemade pallets of twigs and leaves. Young gorillas nest in trees while older gorillas nest on the ground.

Female gorillas begin mating when they reach maturity, which is 7-

10 years old. At that time, they leave their mother's troop and go in search of a mate. Once impregnated, they carry their offspring for nine months. They only have one baby or two at a time. Once born, the baby gorillas will stay attached to their mothers until they are three or four years old. During this time, they will mostly consume their mother's milk. Once they are fully weaned at three or four years old, they will eat the same diet as a mature gorilla. Mother gorillas will fight to the death to protect their young.

FYI: Female gorillas will give birth to 2-6 babies in a lifetime, as a general rule.

The silver-gray in the middle of his back is what earns him the name 'silverback.' This strip doesn't appear until the gorilla reaches maturity, which is when he is twelve years old or so.

Fun Facts...

The arms of a gorilla are longer than their legs.

Primates are highly intelligent. They can use basic tools and learn sign language.

The DNA of gorillas is 98% identical to that of a human. They are the closest living relative to humans after the chimpanzee and the bonobo.

A bonobo was formerly called the Pygmy Chimpanzee

Here is a fascinating fact. *Gorillas don't need to drink water!* They get all the water they need from their water-rich plant diet and the mountain dew.

FYI: Dian Fossey was a famous (and the first) renowned primate researcher and conservationist. She was the first to study mountain gorillas in their natural habitat. She was a great advocate for these primates until her death in 1985. Her life—and tragic death—is a compelling story. The book, *Gorillas in the Mist*, was made into a major motion picture. You can visit her grave in Rwanda.

Gorilla Safaris

You will have a briefing with your guide and later with park officials, so you will learn everything you need to know and have any questions you may have answered. But here are some things you need to know before you go:

Flash photography is not allowed.

You need to be in good shape as the terrain is mountainous and includes prolonged trekking through forests. Also, the altitude and humidity can be challenging if you have any health issues, such as respiratory or heart problems.

You can participate in a gorilla safari year round, but I have already discussed that it is advisable to avoid the rainy seasons. However, it can rain even in the dry season.

It is *essential* that you pack the right gear. I discuss what you need to bring in the packing section of this chapter.

There is never a guarantee that you will see wildlife. However, the trackers are very good, and it is almost unheard of not to see gorillas during your safari.

You must obtain a gorilla permit in advance of arrival in Uganda or Rwanda. You should obtain your permit well in advance of your trip. The number of people allowed into the park each day is limited. If you are using a tour operator, which I highly recommend, they will take care of this for you. If you want to participate in more than one gorilla safari, you can buy additional permits. But you will have to decide on the second safari in advance, as well.

Note: Permit money is used for anti-poaching efforts and habitat conservation.

If you are buying travel insurance (and you should for most trips), you need to inquire if the gorilla permit would be reimbursed if you have to cancel for any reason. While your trip is refundable if you have good insurance, the permits are usually not refundable. Also, some insurers may require an additional premium to be paid for this activity.

There is a minimum age to participate in a gorilla safari, and that is sixteen years old. This is strictly enforced in both Uganda and Rwanda. There is no maximum age so come on so long as you are in good health.

My Gorilla Safari

While you can't go wrong with either place, we chose Uganda for our gorilla safari.

We landed in Entebbe and spent the night in a cozy guest house. We enjoyed sundowners (cocktails) and a wonderful dinner. We went to bed early to rest up for what was ahead.

The next day eight of us boarded a small plane for an hour-long flight to a small airstrip. The flight was smooth, and we saw some scenery on route. (Note: If you don't fly, it is a two-day drive or one very long day). When we landed, our guides and jeeps were waiting for us. We proceeded on our journey, which was an hour or so drive to our camp.

Upon arrival, we were greeted with light refreshments and an in-depth briefing about what to expect on our safari the next day.

Before dinner, we had time to check into our rooms and get freshened up. The treehouses were spread out and were at different levels. Our cottage was perched at the highest level. As we made our first trek, we counted the number of steps—50! Yes, every time we wanted to go back to our room (like if you forgot your jacket or camera), we had to climb up all those steps and then go back down. You had to be careful not to misstep on your way down, especially after dusk. The camp did place lanterns on every landing, which helped.

On the plus side is the amazing

view. I will never forget watching the sunrise and sunset from our balcony (I have included these photos and many others at the back of this book).

That first night, we ate dinner with our driver/guide and then retired to get our gear together for our trek. I will discuss what you need in the packing section later in this reference.

The next morning, we ate a high protein and carb breakfast, grabbed our walking sticks, and headed down to meet our great driver/guide, Joseph. Since our camp was close to the entrance to Bwindi, it was only a five minute walk.

When we entered the park, it was somewhat overwhelming. There were so many people, including other participants, guides, porters, and park officials. We were given a little talk by the park supervisor and then divided into groups of eight. The idea is not to overwhelm the gorillas with big groups. Each group is assigned a guide supervisor and an assistant guide. We parted company with Joseph, who wished us well.

We didn't see the trackers until later as they had already been sent ahead to track the gorillas.

I should mention the importance of porters. It is strictly up to you, but I highly advise it. Your porter will carry your backpack, help you with difficult crossings, and even serve as a cheerleader when you think you can't go on! You pay them a tip at the end of the day. You may pay whatever you want, but the normal amount is $10 - $20. You cannot carry anything in your hands as you need them free to navigate the jungle. Your backpack is a tad heavy as it contains your lunchbox, enough water for the day, camera gear, jacket, and other personal effects. Plus, hiring the guides, trackers, and porters provides revenue for the locals. Your permit money goes toward protecting these animals and their habitat. If not for tourism, these great gorillas would be extinct.

You will be expected to tip the trackers and your guide. Again, this is only a few dollars and money well spent since they get you in and out of the jungle intact and up close to the gorillas without harm.

The duration of your trek depends on many variables. For instance, we got assigned to a gorilla family that was deep in the jungle. Some families are close, and you may only have to trek for thirty minutes. The average trek is two hours.

Also, weather conditions/time of year play a role in how long your trek takes. If the trails are muddy, it takes longer to navigate them. If food is scarce, which it is during the latter part of the dry season, the gorillas have to go deeper into the forest to find it and so do you! Since we went during the dry season because we didn't want to trek in the rain, this was an issue for us. We were also assigned one of the largest and most habituated families, which was good news. The bad news is it was one of the farthest groups to reach.

Another factor is your group. You're only as strong as your weakest link. We had a gal in our group who could not keep up with the group, so we had to stop frequently to wait for her. By the time she caught up to us, the trackers often notified us via walkie-talkie radios that the gorillas were on the move again. This went on for half a day before our guide made the decision that we were going to have to go ahead without this lady. He left an armed game warden, her porter, and an assistant guide with her, and we hurried on our way.

Before our group broke up, we stopped for lunch. This was probably three hours or so into the hike. We ate in a clearing of sorts, sitting on fallen logs and tree stumps. The camp had packed us some fruit, a sandwich, and cookies (Vegetarian options were available).

After about twenty minutes or so, we were told it was time to continue. We put our trash into our lunchboxes and returned our packs to our porters. This was no easy hike. In some places, the guides were using their machetes to clear a path for us. We were climbing straight up a mountain for much of the time and over large fallen trees. We were crossing creeks and pulling ourselves up the mountain on occasion using tree branches. We followed single file up tiny trails and clomped through overgrowth while watching for snakes. And being a jungle, it was humid. I'm talking ninety percent humidity.

Just when we thought we couldn't go on much longer and that

the mountain gorillas were a myth, word trickled back to us that the gorillas were just up ahead. The porters took our walking sticks and stayed put while we silently followed our guide.

We had been told during our briefing that once we got within eyesight of the gorillas we needed to be quiet. Silently, we approached and saw a couple of gorillas eating. And then we saw some more gorillas, including two females with babies clinging to their backs.

And then three juvenile males came thundering past us, but not before two of them stopped and grabbed my leg! The first one grabbed my pants and then kept going. The second one did the same, but lingered a bit longer. The third male ran right past me without stopping. Thankfully, my friend, Jim, did get a shot of second gorilla grabbing me. It is one of the photos in the back of this book. This was the highlight of the whole trip for me. How often do you get groped by a gorilla?!

Suddenly, we heard a noise and our group turned to see the most spectacular sight. The group leader, a massive male silverback was standing on the trail in front of us. There are photos of him and the rest of the troop in the back of this book.

So how it works is that you are allowed thirty minutes with the gorillas. At the end of that time, the guide will signal that it is time to go and you make your journey out of the jungle.

But because of the long, strenuous hike we had (I will tell you just how long at the end of this section) and also because the gal we had to leave behind didn't catch up to us until we had been with the gorillas for twenty minutes or so, the guide allowed us to observe the gorillas for a few more minutes. This was great, but the bad news is that the gorillas began moving—up, of course. So we bravely went straight up the mountain where there were no trails or even footholds. We were literally hanging off the mountain in a couple of places. I remember grabbing onto tree branches so that I wouldn't fall down into the abyss. But the branch broke off in my hand twice! I just said a quick prayer and kept going, just like the rest of the group was doing, I'm sure. This was the most thrilling part of the trek as we were in this very remote place, following these big, beautiful gorillas. I felt a bit like an explorer, deep in the jungle, seeing and doing something extraordinary.

    I promised you I would share our trek time, so here it is. We trekked for 8.5 hours! We were later told this was a record. As I mentioned earlier, most treks take an average of two hours, so this was most unusual. The entire camp cheered upon our return.

    We returned to the park the

next day to get our certificates from our guide. We watched a short video too, which I think would have made more sense on the front end rather than after the fact. But maybe they didn't want to delay us with a video as we had much ground to cover that day!

So in case you're rethinking your gorilla safari plans, let me assure you that I would do it all again. Seeing the gorillas up close was worth it all. In fact, I think it worked out for the best. We got to see more of Bwindi than most gorilla trekkers get to and we enjoyed a rather exhilarating hike. And we saw the biggest gorilla family, which included nearly a dozen gorillas. And you do see the gorillas up close. We were less than five feet away from the farthest gorilla and a foot or so away from the closest one. As I mentioned, I had two touch me and that memory will stay with me forever.

About Gorilla Permits and More You Need to Know…

I want to be sure you realize that the gorilla permits are non-refundable. If you cannot take the trip for whatever reason, you will not get this money back—even if you have travel insurance. You cannot reschedule. Your permit is issued for a certain day and is good for that day only. Your permit is not transferable to someone else. It is in your name, and only you can use it. So if you cannot make the trip, you cannot sell it to someone else who needs a permit.

Another thing you should know about permits is that they cost twice as much in Rwanda as Uganda. If you're wondering if that's because it's a better experience in Rwanda, the answer is no. The government has simply decided that they need to charge more to cover gorilla-related services, such as game wardens and park maintenance.

That said, you may have to venture deeper into Bwindi Impenetrable Forest to find gorillas than you do in Rwanda's Volcanoes National Park. Also, there are a few more gorillas in Rwanda than Uganda. So, on average, treks are shorter in Rwanda than Uganda. However, I have heard of groups finding gorillas in Uganda in less than thirty minutes and groups trekking for more than five hours in Rwanda to find gorillas. Nothing is guaranteed in regards to wildlife watching! The bottom line is that you need to be in good physical shape for this trip. Do some conditioning before your trip by taking long walks or hikes. If you train on a treadmill, be sure to raise the incline to simulate a mountain hike.

The reason I prefer Uganda is

that the country is much larger than Rwanda, so it has more parks (more wildlife!) and lots of other things to see and do.

You should also be aware that guides have total authority. If they decide you cannot go on the trek or say you must turn back, then you must do so. For example, if you have any infectious illness (like a cold), the guide will probably not let you go. Gorillas are highly susceptible to human diseases.

If we hadn't reached the gorillas when we did, we were at great risk of having to turn around and head back so as not to be stumbling around in the jungle in the dark.

There is little danger from the gorillas as they are herbivores. They will not bother you unless the silverback (group leader) deems you are a threat.

Also, two game wardens accompany every group. We lost one of our armed guards when he had to stay with the lady we left behind. But we still had one armed guard. And this was an unusual situation as I'm told they won't normally separate a group like that.

Another thing I'd like to mention is regarding your time with the gorillas. It is tempting to keep taking pictures, but you shouldn't. Last season, I interviewed a gal for my show who had completed a Rwanda gorilla trek, and she advised me to allow some time to just watch the gorillas. I remembered that piece of advice and stopped taking pictures after about fifteen minutes. I had probably already taken forty or fifty photos by that time so I think that was plenty! I spent the rest of the time just watching them interact with each other and it was such a remarkable experience. I am so grateful for that advice. I share the link to that episode of *Terrance Talks Travel: Über*

Adventures at the back of the book if you'd like to hear more about gorilla safaris.

About Accommodations…

If you are putting together your trip rather than using a tour company, you will have to make arrangements for lodging. There are several choices in Uganda's Bwindi area, ranging from budget to deluxe, such as Buhoma Lodge, Silverback Lodge, Engagi Lodge, Eco Marvels Gorilla Resort, Jungle View Lodge, Gorilla Friends Lodge, and Bwindi Guest House.

FYI: There is a luxury camp *inside* Bwindi Impenetrable Forest. Sanctuary Gorilla Forest Camp is the only camp inside the park. It is very nice and also very expensive. To be honest, I don't think it is worth the extra money. Our camp, Buhoma Lodge, was pretty great and located just outside the park entrance. That said, on occasion,

gorillas do venture into the Sanctuary Gorilla Forest Camp since it is inside the park. There is video footage of such an occasion on their website,
http://www.sanctuaryretreats.com/uganda-camps-gorilla-forest

In Rwanda's Volcanoes National Park, options range from budget to deluxe, as well. Some popular places include Sabyinyo Silver Back Lodge, Virunga Lodge, Mountain Gorilla View Lodge and Gorillas Nest Lodge, Gorillas Volcanoes Hotel, Le Bambou Gorilla Lodge, La Palme Hotel, Muhabura Hotel, Kinigi, Villa Gorilla, Carr Hotel, Red Rock and Rwanda.

About Rwanda

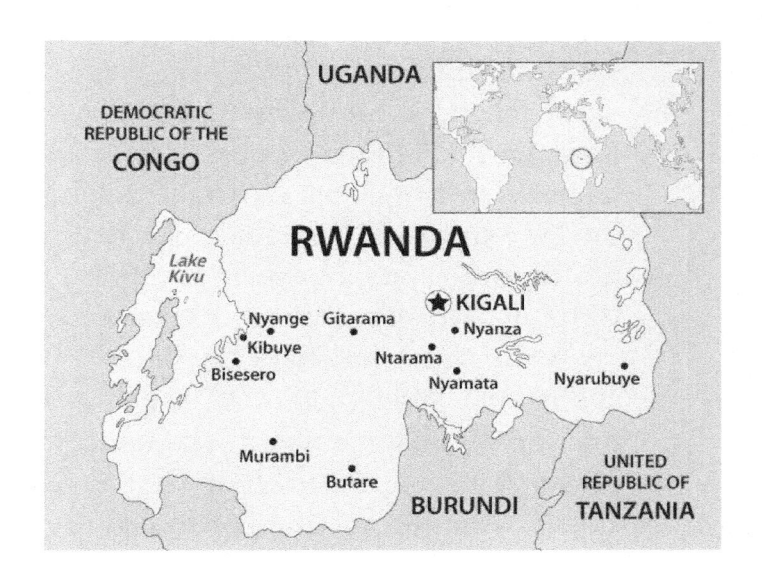

Tribal peoples have inhabited Rwanda for thousands of years. The Tutsi were the upper class or royalty, and the Hutu were the lower class or working class. The Tutsi owned the land while the Hutu farmed it. A Tutsi King, Mwami, ruled the people.

The first European to visit Rwanda was German Count Von Goetzen in 1894. Just five years later, the Mwami made Rwanda a German protectorate state. However, by 1915, Belgium was in control of Rwanda.

By 1959, the Hutu revolted against the Tutsi monarchy. They overthrew the government and took power. This was a dark time for the Tutsis. Many were killed or forced to flee their country.

Rwanda gained its independence from Belgium on July 1, 1962.

In 1990, a full-scale civil war between the Tutsis and the Hutus was going on. Within four years things had escalated to an even more disasterous state. What has become known as the Rwandan Genocide was occurring.

The Hutu government tried to eradicate all Tutsis. Once again, the Tutsis were forced to flee or be killed. From April 7 to mid-July 1994, an estimated 500,000–1,000,000 Rwandans were killed with most of those deaths being Tutsi and accounting for about twenty percent of Rwanda's population.

By the time this horrific war was over, Rwanda's economy was in ruin. It has taken many years for things to stabilize and reconstruction and reconciliation are still ongoing.

Today, approximately eighty percent of the population is Hutu, and about twenty percent are Tutsi.

The Rwandan president is elected by the people every seven years. It is interesting to note that the Rwanda Parliament has more female members than any other parliament in the world.

Rwanda is officially called the Republic of Rwanda. It is one of the smallest countries in Africa that is not an island nation. It is situated just a few degrees south of the Equator, so it is in the Southern Hemisphere.

Rwanda is the most densely populated country in Africa with a population of close to thirteen million with roughly one million of its inhabitants living in its capital, Kigali.

Unlike other African countries, there are no villages in Rwanda. Instead, there are communities full of individual family farms.

Everyone in Rwanda has to take part in their service program, including the president. On the last Saturday of every month, there is a day of mandatory national community service called Umuganda. This has helped rebuild the country after the Rwandan Genocide. Medical centers, schools, and agricultural centers have been built largely through volunteerism.

The economy is based primarily on agriculture with coffee and tea being the major exports. Tourism is also a huge source of revenue for this small nation because Rwanda is one of only two countries where mountain gorillas can safely be seen in the wild.

Rwanda Historical Timeline

1858 - British explorer Hanning Speke is the first European to visit the area.

1890 - Rwanda becomes part of German East Africa.

1916 - Belgian forces occupy Rwanda.

1959 - The Tutsi King *Mwami* died and riots broke out with the Hutu majority fighting against the Tutsi aristocracy.

1961 - Before the violence had entirely died away, the first pre-independence elections were held and won by the Hutu Emancipation Movement, known as PARMEHUTU.

1962 - Rwanda became independent from Belgium, even though both were ethnically and cultural united. Burundi's first government was controlled by Tutsi while the first Rwandan government was Hutu.

1962-1963: From bases in western Uganda, Tutsi refugees launched attacks into Rwanda.

1963-1964 - More violence caused thousands of Tutsi to flee to Burundi, Uganda and Tanzania, but they failed to integrate into their new countries. The

Rwanda government refused to allow them to return.

1973 - General Juvenal Habyarimana seized power in Rwanda in a military coup. He was a Hutu.

1975 - Habyarimana declared a one-party state under the MRND as a way to overcome ethnic divisions. A system of quotas was devised to limit Tutsi participation in civil service jobs.

1975 - France signed its first "Technical Military Assistance Agreement (TMAA) with Rwanda.

1987 - Coffee prices collapsed, crushing the Rwandan economy.

1990s - Drought hit several regions of Rwanda and some people were unable to buy food, so many died.

1990 - A civil war began when the Rwandan Patriotic Front invaded from Uganda. Many Rwandans saw this as an attempt to re-establish the colonial-era government. France increased its military support to the Rwandan government. More than 700,000 people were made homeless and the government increased its repressive measures in order to stifle opposition.

1992 - Habiyarimana formed a multiparty government headed by prime minister Dismas Nsengiyaremye.

1993 - Second invasion of Rwanda from Uganda by Rwandan Patriotic Front troops.

1993 - The Arusha Peace Accord was signed but never implemented due to opposition from hard-line members of Habyarimana's government.

1993 - The United Nations authorized a peacekeeping force (UNAMIR) to monitor the Arusha Peace Accord process.

1994 - A French airplane, *Mystere-Falcon*, was shot down, killing Presidents Juvenal Habyarimana of Rwanda and Cyprien Ntaryamira of Burundi. A UN investigation blamed the shooting on the Rwandan presidential guard, who immediately spread out through Kigali to hunt down pro-democracy politicians. Among the dead were democratic politicians and Prime

Minister Agathe Uwilingiyimana, a Hutu and one of the first African women vice-presidents. Food aid distribution to 700,000 refugees in the north ceased.

1994 - Violence broke out with armed gangs of thugs responsible for killing Tutsis, including many women and children.

1994 - The Rwandan Patriotic Front (Tutsi rebel movement based in Uganda) launched an offensive against the Rwandan capital of Kigali. Government forces launched counter-operations that targeted Tutsis. French soldiers landed and secured the Kigali Airport without notifying the UN. Theodore Sindikubwabo declared himself president of an interim Rwandan "Hutu Power" government.

1994 - The RPF ordered the remaining French and Belgians to get out of Kigali.

1994 - The French completed the evacuation of 1,361 people including 450 French nationals and 178 Rwandan officials and their families.

1994 - US President Clinton issued Presidential Decision Directive (PDD 25) which required a clear statement of

American interests, the approval of Congress, availability of funds, a specific date for withdrawal, and an agreed-upon command and control structure the requirement for the commitment of American military resources overseas.

1994 -The RPF declared a unilateral ceasefire, but by then more than 800,000 were dead and many more were refugees.

1994 - French President Mitterand announced a new effort in Rwanda called Operation Turquoise.

1994 - The French agreed to ship a military force to Rwanda via Goma and Bukavu (Zaire) and the border post at Cyangungu at the southern end of Lake Kivu.

1994 - Kigali fell to RPF forces.

1994 - Ruhengiri fell to RPF forces.

1994 - Gisenyi fell to RPF forces. In the next four days, an unprecedented 1.2 million people crossed the border into Zaire where

UN staff (UNHCR) had made preparations for only about 50,000 refugees.

1994 - The new RPF government was sworn into office in Kigali.

1994 -The new prime minister Faustin Twagiramungu announced plans to prosecute up to 30,000 people for the genocide.

1994 - Operation Turquoise ended and French troops left. The first Canadian troops arrived in Kigali.

Today - Rwanda is still recovering from its civil war in 1990s and rebuilding its economy, with coffee and tea production among its main exports. The World Bank has praised Rwanda's "remarkable development successes."

Some interesting facts about Rwanda...

Plastic bags are illegal due to the harm they do to the environment.

Flip flops are also illegal.

It is frowned upon to walk on manicured lawns.

The average life expectancy is 50 years old (Some sources say 40 and other sources say 60).

Rwanda is leading Africa's digital revolution. The Smart Kigali Initiative is bringing free wireless internet to most public places, including on public buses, hospitals, taxi parks, offices, and restaurants.

The Karisimbi Volcano in the Virunga Mountains is the highest point in Rwanda.

You can travel from one end of this country to the other end in less than four hours!

The Kigali Convention Center, which cost $300 million (U.S. dollars), is the most expensive building in Africa.

* * *

About Uganda

The first white man to visit was explorer Henry Stanley in 1875. Anglican missionaries arrived in 1877 and then came the Roman Catholic missionaries in 1879. But the Ugandans didn't take these attempts to convert them to Christianity well. For example, Bishop James Hannington was murdered in 1885.

Just a few years later, the British East Africa Company was given control of Uganda by the British monarchy. The local chiefs were rendered powerless. By 1894, the British government declared Uganda to be one of its colonies. This meant the country was under the total control of the British.

Cotton was introduced in the

early 1900s. By 1914, it was a major export of Uganda. By the early 1920s, coffee and tea were grown here. They also became major exports.

Uganda continued to grow with new schools and a railway being built. Executive and legislative councils were formed.

By the 1940s and 1950s, a hydroelectric plant had opened, and mining operations had begun. Uganda was growing at a rapid rate thanks to coffee, cotton, and tea exports.

But the Ugandans were tired of another country deciding their fate and claiming much of their money. There was an uprising, and by October 9, 1962, Uganda had reclaimed its independence. There was now a president and a prime minister.

But once again this African nation was thrown into turmoil when the prime minister staged a coup and ousted the president. He became a dictator and did nothing to help Uganda or its people. Just a few years into Obote's rule, he was overthrown by Idi Amin. Sadly, Amin was worse than his predecessor. He was a total tyrant who murdered more than 100,000 Ugandans. Many of these people were tortured and beaten to death. Amin forced all the Asians living in Uganda to leave, but he confiscated their assets beforehand.

Many of the Asians were businessmen. Soon after their departure, the Ugandan economy collapsed. Furthermore, Amin did not take care of the country's infrastructure, so that further led to Uganda's demise.

In another disastrous move, Amin attacked Tanzania in 1978. Tanzania retaliated by invading Uganda and defeating Amin's military. Amin fled the country and was never brought to justice before his death.

Unbelievably, Obote once again ended up as prime minister. And once again, Obote set his sights on the presidency. He imprisoned anyone who disagreed with him and kept a tight fist on the media. If any reporter said or wrote anything he didn't like, he expelled them from the country.

The National Resistance Army ran Obote and his supporters out in 1986. A new president was elected, and soon things were changing for the better. Uganda was stabilizing and starting to grow and prosper once again. The Asians who had been expelled by Obote began to return. By 2005, there were political parties and the people were able to live and vote as they liked.

Uganda is officially the Republic of Uganda, which I thought was pronounced ew-gan-da until I got there and discovered it is yoo-ga(h)-

de. It is bordered to the east by Kenya, to the west by the DRC (Congo), to the north by Sudan, to the southwest by Rwanda and the south by Tanzania. It shares Lake Victoria with Kenya and Tanzania.

The largest city is the capital, Kampala, which has been named the 13th fastest growing city on the planet, with an annual population growth rate of four percent. Kampala has been voted the best city to live in East Africa—even ahead of Nairobi and Dodoma. It is divided into five boroughs: Kampala Central Division, Kawempe Division, Makindye Division, Nakawa Division, and Rubaga Division.

The tallest building in Kampala, The Pearl of Africa Hotel Kampala, was completed in 2017 after nearly a dozen years under construction. But it may soon be dethroned by the 34-story Kampala Intercontinental Hotel (nicknamed the Kingdom Hotel Kampala), which is currently under construction. Surrounding Kampala is the rapidly growing Wakiso District, whose population more than doubled between 2004 and 2014, growing from less than one million to more than two million today.

Most Ugandans grow their own food unless they live in a large urban area, such as Kampala and Entebbe. Typically, only two meals are consumed a day: lunch and supper. Breakfast is a cup of tea or a small bowl of porridge. The meals are prepared by mothers and daughters, not sons or fathers. In fact, boys and men do not even enter the kitchen, which is separate from the house because cooking is done on an open wood fire. Popular dishes are matoke (a fish and bananas entree), millet bread, chicken or beef stew, and cassava. Pumpkin, yams, goat meat, fish, papayas, millet, white potatoes, pineapple, beans, and groundnuts are often used in dishes. The national drink is Waragi, which is a gin made from bananas. A popular dish with Ugandans is fried grasshoppers.

Like Rwanda, the primary economy is agriculture and tourism. Since rivers and lakes constitute more than twenty percent of Uganda's land, fishing is also an important industry. Thanks to the mountain gorillas, tourism is becoming a significant revenue source, as well.

Uganda Historical Timeline

- 1800s - Buganda gains control over the western shores of Lake Victoria
- 1862 - John Hanning Speke, a British explorer, is the first European visitor to the area.
- 1870s - Protestant missionaries from England and Catholic missionaries from France to begin work in Uganda.
- 1885-1891, Period of the martyrs of Buganda who were killed for their steadfast Christian faith. They refused to offer sacrifices to the traditional gods

and objected to King Mwanga's homosexual practices. Martyrs day is now celebrated on June 3. A four-year religious revolt began in 1888, which the Protestants won in 1892.
- 1890 - A treaty is signed by Britain and Germany giving Britain rights to what was to become Uganda.
- 1892 - British East India Company exerts influence in Uganda to help the Protestant missionaries defeat their Catholic counterparts.
- 1893 - The British Union Jack is raised over the Kingdom of Buganda. The British mistakenly drop the letter "B" from the name and calls their new acquision "Uganda."
- 1894 (April 11) - Uganda was declared a British protectorate largely to protect the source of the Nile. Winston Churchill visits and calls it "The Pearl of Africa." The town of Entebbe was the capital of the protectorate until 1962.
- 1900 - Britain signs agreement with Buganda giving it autonomy and turning it into a constitutional monarchy controlled mostly by Protestants.

- 1904 - Cultivation of cotton for export begins.
- 1954 - Introduction of hydroelectric power with construction of Ownes Falls Dam at what is now known as Jinji.
- 1958 - Internal self-government is allowed.
- 1962 - Uganda begins self-government, with Benedicto Kiwanuka as prime minister.
- 1962 - Uganda gains independence after nearly 70 years of British rule.
- 1962 - Uganda is admitted as a member of the United Nations.
- 1967- A new constitution makes Uganda a republic.
- 1971 - A former private in the Ugandan army, Idi Amin, seizes power in a military coup and overthrows Milton Obote.
- 1972 - President Idi Amin expels all Asians with British passports, forcing them to leaving most of their possessions and businesses behind. This led to the collapse of the economy of Uganda.
- 1972 – Amin told the people that Tanzanian forces (later reported to be Ugandan exiles who opposed Idi Amin's government) had crossed the border and captured three Ugandan towns before being driven out by Amin's troops.

- 1972 - Idi Amin nationalized forty-one foreign-owned farms and tea estates, of which thirty-four were British. This eventually led to the expulsion of all foreign business interests from Uganda. The country is still recovering from this act.
- 1976 - Palestinian extremists hijacked Air France Flight 139 in Greece with 246 passengers and 12 crew. The flight eventually landed at Entebbe Airport because Idi Amin offered them safe passage.
- 1976 – Israeli Commando raided Entebbe Airport to free Israeli highjack victims from Air France Flight 139
- 1976 - After four years of tension with the government of Idi Amin, Britain broke off diplomatic relations with Uganda. It had been 30 years since the British government had taken such a drastic step against another country.
- April 1979 - Tanzania invades Uganda, forcing Amin to flee the country. Yusufu Lule is installed as president, but is quickly replaced by Godfrey Binaisa.

- 1980 - Godfrey Binaisa is overthrown by the army and Milton Obote becomes president.
- 1985 - Obote is deposed in military coup and is replaced by Tito Okello.
- 1986 - After years of civil war in which hundreds of thousands are either killed or are displaced, Yoweri Museveni's National Resistance Army takes power. Under his leadership, Uganda has steadily achieved economic growth, the rebuilding of the shattered infrastructure, a free press and judicial system, and peace in most part of the country.
- 1989 - Joseph Kony leads an armed revolt in the north against Museveni. Kony's group is known as the "LRA" (Lord's Resistance Army), but his brutality eventually led to the loss of local support.
- 1993 - President Museveni restored traditional kings, but with no political power.
- 1995 – A new constitution is adopted but maintains a ban on political activity.
- 1996 - Uganda held its first presidential election in sixteen years. President Yoweri Museveni won, thanks to his ten-year effort to restore peace and democracy since the end of the civil war.

- 1997 - Ugandan Peoples Defense Force deposes Mobutu Sese Seko of Zaire, who is replaced by Laurent Kabila.
- 1998 - UDPF helps rebels overthrow Kabila.
- 1999 - Rwandan Hutu rebels killed eight foreign tourists (gorilla trackers at Bwindi Impenetrable Forest) they had kidnaped the day before. The U.S. arrested three rebels for this crime in March of 2003.
- 2001 - Uganda classifies Rwanda, a former ally in the war in the Congo, a hostile nation due to fighting in 2000 between the two countries in the Democratic Republic of Congo.
- 2001 - President Museveni wins another term.
- 2002 - Uganda signs an agreement with Sudan seeking to shut down the rebel group, Lord's Resistance Army (LRA). The LRA, led by their "prophet," have kidnapped thousands of children and displaced many civilians.
- 2002 - Peace deal signed with Uganda National Rescue Front rebels after more than five years of negotiations.

- 2003 - Uganda pulls the last of its troops from eastern Democratic Republic of Congo and tens of thousands of civilians seek safety in Uganda.
- 2004 - Government and LRA rebels hold their first face-to-face talks, but there is no breakthrough in ending the insurgency.
- Today - Uganda remains stable and many improvements have been seen, such as free primary education and successful HIV/AIDS campaigns. Agriculture continues to boost the local economy, with Uganda's coffee, cotton, and tea being exported all over the world. Tourism has increased and Uganda is becoming known for its hospitality.

Some interesting facts about Uganda...

There is an interesting law in Uganda. If you cut down a tree, you must plant three trees in its place. I wish we had that law here in America.

Half the population of Uganda is under the age of 14, which makes it the world's youngest country. Like Rwanda, life expectancy is low—an average of 50 years old.

You will see far more bicycles and boda-bodas (motorbikes) in

Uganda than vehicles.

In Uganda, "skimpy" is defined as "not reaching your ankles."

The average church service in Uganda lasts 4-6 hours!

Pan-fried grasshoppers are a delicacy and local favorite in Uganda.

* * *

Uganda Safari Parks

There are many more parks in Uganda than Rwanda. These are discussed in the next section, but here is quick rundown:

*Bwindi Impenetrable Forest=gorillas

Kibale Forest=chimpanzees

Kidepo Valley NP=least visited but good chance of seeing some animals that are not commonly seen in this region, such as cheetahs.

Lake Mburo=smallest park but the most safari options

Mgahinga Gorilla NP=gorillas and scenic views

Murchison Falls NP=largest park

*Queen Elizabeth NP=tree-climbing lions & best wildlife viewing

Rwenzori NP=hiking

Semuliki NP=birding and hot springs

*   *   *

Uganda Highlights:

*Gorilla & Chimp tracking

*Queen Elizabeth National Park (home to rare tree-climbing lions)

*Lake Victoria sunset cruise

*Kazinga Channel Boat Safari

*Kampala

*Crossing the Equator

*Rafting on the Nile at Jinja

http://visituganda.com/

Uganda Attractions

Batwa Experience. If you're up for a long hike, you may choose to visit the remote village of the Batwa Pygmies or enjoy a two-hour Batwa Experience. This tribe was the first to live in this part of Africa. They were hunters and gatherers. Unfortunately, they hunted gorillas for food and to sell to poachers. The government has had to intercede to protect the gorillas. They paid the Batwa *not* to hunt the gorillas. They had some success with this arrangement. However, the gorillas sometimes got ensnared in traps the Batwas set to catch other animals for food, so they were ultimately relocated outside the parks in the early 1990s. For a fee, the Batwa invite tourists into their community and show them how they live, how they make medicines, and so forth. They also sell handicrafts.

Bwindi Impenetrable Forest is the best place for a gorilla trek. It is also home to several other primate species, such as the chimpanzee, olive baboon, and Colobus monkey. Bwindi also boasts the largest population of birds and butterflies.

Entebbe Botanical Gardens is home to lots of birds, monkeys, and a few other animals (mostly insects) and some flora and fauna.

Jinga is the fabled source of the Nile River. Located at Lake Victoria, a town has sprung up as a hub for adventure travelers. Whitewater rafting, kayaking, bungee jumping, ATV expeditions, horseback riding, jet boating, mountain biking, and sunset cruises can be accomplished here. Several outfitters can be found here, such as the Nile River Explorers, www.raftafrica.com.

Nile River at Jinga

FYI: You can also go fishing here. We caught Nile Perch, and our camp cook served them for dinner!

Kampala. Located near the shores of Africa's largest lake, Lake Victoria, Uganda's capital city boasts many bars, restaurants, and nightclubs. It is a great place to begin or end your wildlife adventure. Kampala is also the largest city in Uganda and is one of the fastest growing cities in the world. A city tour is a good way to get oriented and learn about local attractions, such as the Uganda Museum, Lubiri Palace, and Kasabi Tombs.

Kibale National Park is the #1 spot for chimpanzee tracking in Uganda. But be warned that they can be harder to find than the mountain gorillas. But there are a dozen other primates that can be found in this park. Butterflies and birds are also abundant.

Kidepo Valley National Park is the most remote park in Uganda, so it is the least visited. This is a shame because it offers pristine beauty and exceptional wildlife viewing. There are two dozen species of mammals. Some of these cannot be found elsewhere in Uganda, such as the black-backed jackal, Burchell's Zebra, Rothschild's Giraffe, and several species of antelopes. Until its recent extinction, the black rhino could be found here.

Lake Mburo National Park.
Although it is the smallest park, it is among the prettiest in Uganda. It also offers a wide variety of safari options, including mountain bike, horseback, boat, jeep, and walking. It is also one of the few parks to offer night game drives, which increases the odds of leopard sightings. Other wildlife commonly seen include Defassa Waterbucks, Oribis, warthogs, hippos, elands, giraffes, and Burchell's Zebras (only place in Uganda where they can be found other than Kidepo.)

Lake Victoria is home to dozens of world-class resorts and more than 150 tourist areas (including heritage sites). The lake is approximately 400,000 years old. The lake is so large that it borders three countries, including Kenya, Tanzania, and Uganda. In fact, it is Africa's largest tropical lake and the second largest freshwater lake in the world. The lake is used to generate hydroelectricity. A visit to the Entebbe Botanical Gardens located on the lake's shores and a sunset boat ride are popular tourist activities.

Mgahinga Gorilla National Park in the Virunga Mountains offers gorilla tracking but is inferior to Bwindi because there are far fewer gorillas. Furthermore, the nomadic gorillas sometimes cross the border so sightings are not as reliable as Bwindi. However, the park is high up in the mountainous region that borders the Congo and Rwanda, so the view is one of the best in Uganda. It is also home to many birds, the endangered Golden Monkey, and features three extinct volcanoes. On the negative side, it sees more rain and is colder than anywhere else in the country.

Murchison Falls National Park began as a game reserve in 1926 but was established as a national park in 1952. It is the country's oldest and largest conservation area. Located in the Rift Valley, the park extends nearly 1,500 square miles (3,800km). The Nile River flows through a narrow gorge at Murchison Falls before dropping into the 'Devil's Cauldron.' It is home to lots of wildlife (76 mammal species), such as leopards, lions, baboons, cheetahs, hippos, Nile crocodiles, colobus monkeys, chimpanzees, and more than 500 species of birds. The biggest population of Rothschild Giraffes (also known as Uganda or Baringo Giraffes)—up to 1,000—are in this park. River cruises are a way to get close-up to the falls, which are among the most impressive in East Africa.

FYI: The legendary 1951 film "The African Queen" starring Humphrey Bogart was filmed on in Murchison Falls National Park.

Ngamba Island Chimpanzee Sanctuary is located on an island at Lake Victoria. Visitors are welcome, but reservations are required. This is where you should go if you want to guarantee chimp sightings. Different packages are available, ranging from a half-day to overnight. The sanctuary's enclosures permit close-up viewing, which is even better at feeding times. In addition to these primates, birds, lizards, bats, and birds can be seen.

Queen Elizabeth National Park is home to all the Big Five except rhinos. This diverse park is the only place where tree-climbing lions can be found. The lions love fig trees found in certain areas of the park and spend most afternoons sleeping high up in these trees. If your guide is good, you can get fairly close without disturbing them. A boat safari on Kazinga Channel is a must with more wildlife sightings than you can imagine.

Rwenzori Mountains are known as "Mountains of the Moon." This mountain range is one of the best trekking destinations in all of Africa. Hikers will enjoy a climb up snow-capped peaks and glaciers, as well as bamboo forests and valley lakes.

Semuliki National Park doesn't have much wildlife, but it is a birdwatcher's paradise with many species of beautiful and exotic birds. Also, there is chimp tracking, nearby hot springs, and Pygmy village.

Ssese Islands is an archipelago of 84 secluded islands clustered around Lake Victoria. They are known as the "Hidden Islands." These islands boast beautiful beaches and lots of privacy. Reading, relaxing, nature walks, nightly bonfires, star gazing, dinners on the beach, village visits, fishing, and canoeing are popular past times. Swimming is not recommended because of hippos and crocodiles.

Uganda Wildlife Education Center is a zoo and conservation center along Lake Victoria.

Victoria Mall is Entebbe's first mall, and while small in comparison to most American malls, it has a food court, some shops, a café, gym, and theatre.

Ziwa Rhino Sanctuary is on the way to Murchison Falls National Park. Participants can track rare rhinos on foot and often get quite close to the animals. Guided treks are led by rangers who also point out other things of interest, such as birds, insects, flora, and fauna. The excursion includes a canoe ride in the refuge's swamp

More Things to Do...

Adventurous souls may choose to visit the **Snake Park**, which is a short

drive from Entebbe. You will get close up to lots of vipers.

Where to Stay…

There are a surprising number of options for lodging in and around Entebbe and Kampala. You can stay in budget accommodations, such as the Gorilla African Guest House, Serene Guesthouse, or Kampala's Forest Cottages. Or you can stay in a five-star hotel, such as Entebbe's Imperial Resort Beach Hotel, Kampala Serena Hotel or Lake Victoria Serena Golf Resort & Spa. Whether you choose budget or deluxe, the accommodations are quite satisfactory. If you book a gorilla safari with a local company or tour operator, lodging is usually included in your package.

Rwanda Highlights:

*Gorilla tracking

*Exploring the Congo Nile Trail

*Hiking the Virunga Volcanoes

*Chimpanzee tracking

*Kigali

https://rwanda-tourism.com/

Rwanda Attractions

Akagera National Park, named after the Akagera River, dates back to 1934 and is considered to have the most diverse and magnificent landscape in East Africa. The park is largely comprised of wetlands, so it has a large number of swamp endemic species, as well as many mammals. These include Topi, Eland, Roan Bush Buck, Impalas, Duikers, Waterbucks, elephants, buffalos, Oribi, Klipspringer, lions, hyenas, leopards, jackals, hippos, and zebras. There are primates here too, including blue monkeys and olive baboons. There are also many species of birds, including a few rare species. The nearly extinct black rhino is being reintroduced. Boat safaris are the best way to spot wildlife in Akagera.

Congo Nile Trail was established in 2009. It's a network of roads and trails that extend from Gisenyi to Cyangugu. Since it runs through rural areas, it is a good chance to see villages, meet locals, and enjoy the scenic landscape. Birders will spot white-breasted cormorants, black-headed herons, white-tailed blue flycatchers, and more. The best option is on a bicycle, but you can walk or rent a motorcycle. You can go on your own or use a guide.

Kigali Farmers and Artisans Market originated in 2017. It began with only a handful of vendors but now has nearly 100. It is a marketplace for art and crafts, food, and food products, with an emphasis on locally grown and raised agricultural products. There is a small entrance fee.

Kigali Genocide Memorial is the final resting place for more than 250,000 victims of the Genocide against the Tutsi in Rwanda. It honors the memory of the more than one million Rwandans killed in 1994 through education and peace-building.

Nyungwe Forest National Park is in the southernmost corner of Rwanda. The park is a rainforest, so its wildlife includes animals that are not commonly found in Africa. A rainforest safari is just as exciting as a safari into the bush. You must look up, down, and all around to find its 200+ species and appreciate all that flora and fauna. There are lovely waterfalls and the oldest and tallest trees in Africa can be found here, including ebonies and mahoganies. Giant tree ferns, orchids, and lobelias are just a few of the plants you'll see here. You can expect to see many species of birds and butterflies, chimpanzees, Colobus Monkeys, red-tailed monkeys, Grey-cheeked Mangabey, L'Hoest Monkeys, Olive Baboons, and more.

Volcanoes National Park is the biggest park in Rwanda, thanks to a significant expansion in 2018. This was done to provide a bigger habitat for its star residents—the mountain gorillas. The additional seventy acres the gorillas get to roam is thanks to the Rwanda Development Board (who manages the park), African Wildlife Foundation, and Wilderness Safaris. Located on the northern tip of Rwanda, this park is biodiverse with everything from lowland forests to alpine forests that are nearly 17,000 feet (5,000 meters) above sea level.

The park, roughly a two-hour drive from Kigali, is on the Rwandan side of the Virunga Mountains, which are shared by Rwanda, Uganda and the Democratic Republic of Congo. In addition to gorillas, the park is home to forest elephants, giant forest hogs, hyenas, duikers, forest buffalos, and other primates. While Volcanoes doesn't have as many bird species as Bwindi, it is home to many birds, and some cannot be found anywhere else in East Africa.

The park, its inhabitants, and tourism suffered during Rwanda's civil war. It was 1999 before it was safe for tourists to return to the place where Dian Fossey happily lived while she studied the mountain gorillas. In 2005, the government began an annual baby gorilla naming ceremony known as "Kwita Iziina."

More things to do…

The adventurous can climb the Virunga Volcanoes. Mount Muhavura is the most accessible peak and can be climbed in one long day.

There is also chimpanzee tracking, but this requires a lengthy trek through rugged terrain. The best place to go is Nyungwe Forest National Park. Be aware that chimps move fast, so it is a challenge to catch up with them. You must be in good physical shape, persistent, and patient!

FYI: More than $16 million in revenue was generated in 2016 from gorilla tourism.

* * *

How To Speak Like A Local

I try to learn some phrases and common words wherever I travel.

Here is a list of common terms that will have you speaking like a local:

Here are some words in Rwanda's official language, Kinyarwanda. Some Rwandans also speak French or English.

Mwaramutse. (Good morning)
Bite? (How are you?)
Muraho (Hello)
Witwande? (What's your name?)
Nitwa ... (My name is ...)
Murakoze. (Thank you)

Some helpful phrases to know in Swahili:

Habari (Hello)

Kwaheri (Goodbye)
Nisaidie, tafadhali (Help me, please!)
Moto (Hot)
Chakula (Food)
Kinywaji (Drink)
Maji (Water)
Asante (Thank you)

*   *   *

FYI: Safari is a Swahili word, which means 'journey.' You will journey into a new place unlike any you've ever seen before; full of wonderful wildlife and amazing scenery—and some of the friendliest people in the world.

Important Information

TIPPING: Most Africans who work in the tourism sector depend on tips. Their wages are low, and they work hard to please visitors. You'll see! Regarding tipping staff in your lodge, camp, or hotel/guesthouse, suggested amounts will be provided to you by management and your tour guide and probably posted in your room or on your travel documents from your tour operator. As a general rule, you should tip ten to twenty percent of your bill. If a staff member has gone the extra mile, feel free to give him/her more money.

TRAVEL DOCUMENTS:

Be sure to keep a copy of your itinerary and emergency contact information with you at all times. Keep copies of every ticket and confirmation to show if needed. You must have a valid passport to enter any country in Africa.

You will need a tourist visa to enter Uganda and Rwanda. This visa can be obtained in advance of your departure or upon arrival at the Uganda or Rwanda airports.

For more on passports and visas,

http://www.passportsandvisas.com/

Give a copy of your itinerary including contact information to a relative or close friend. You may also want to consider checking in with your embassy. The government has a free service called STEP or Smart Traveler Enrollment Program. U.S. citizens and nationals traveling abroad can sign up before leaving the States. The benefits include:

> Receive important information from the Embassy about safety conditions in your destination country, helping you make informed decisions about your travel plans. Help the U.S. Embassy contact you in an emergency, whether natural disaster, civil unrest, or family emergency. Help family and friends get in touch with you in an

emergency.
https://step.state.gov/step/

TRAVEL INSURANCE: Anytime you travel outside of the U.S. (especially adventure trips), I recommend travel insurance. Do a little research or ask your travel agent for recommendations. A good resource is www.insuremytrip.com. This third party resource reveals a reputable list of insurance providers and costs.

TRAVEL WARNINGS: At the time of publication, there were no travel risks for these countries. However, things can change, so it is best to go to http://travel.state.gov for the latest news. Also, be sure to check on the latest regarding visas, passports, and required (and recommended) inoculations.

Vaccine

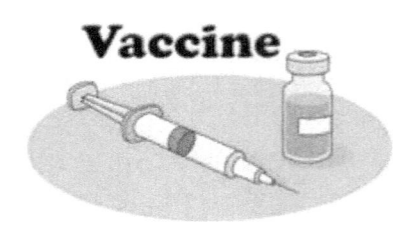

VACCINATIONS: A yellow fever vaccination is required to enter Rwanda and Uganda. You may be asked to show a yellow fever certificate, which is issued by your local county health department after you have received the inoculation. It used to be that the certificate was only valid for ten years, but officials are now saying that the certificate is good for life. So you are good to go so long as you still have your certificate. Since things are always changing, be sure to confirm this with your tour operator or state department. A polio vaccination is required if you are traveling with children under the age of five. Please remember that you must be at least sixteen years old to

participate in a gorilla safari.
http://www.vaccines.gov/travel/ and
http://wwwnc.cdc.gov/travel

FOOD & WATER: Tap water is not safe to drink or even use to brush your teeth in Uganda and Rwanda. Always drink bottled water except in camp where they will provide you with safe drinking water. They will also put a pitcher in your bathroom so that you can use that to brush your teeth. Keep your mouth closed in the shower.

Food is just something you have to use common sense about consuming. You want to try new things, after all, that is the point of travel. But at the same time, you might not be excited about pigeon pie or monkey brains. If something looks or smells or tastes disagreeable, don't eat it. I always travel with protein bars, just in case.

THE PEOPLE: It goes without saying—yet I am saying it because it is such an important point—travelers should always be respectful of other cultures. Not only are you a guest in their country, but you are also an ambassador to your homeland. Your behavior reflects on all people of your native country. Not only should your behavior be exemplary, but you should also dress appropriately.

SAFETY: As with any travel, you are putting yourself out there. Despite any attempts you make, it will probably be obvious that you are a tourist so be sure to exercise common sense. Look around. Pay attention. Don't wander off down a dark, side street alone. If you're out and about and notice that you have entered a desolate or seedy-looking area, hightail it back to a congested area. Don't count your money on the street corner. Don't wear expensive jewelry. Don't call attention to yourself. Don't carry much money with you each day. Don't put your wallet in your back pocket or carry a purse. Be careful to safeguard your passport and other travel documents.

Kampala and Kigali are as safe as most cities, but Entebbe has a high crime rate. You need to exercise caution if you go out alone to explore this city.

ATTITUDE: Traveling can be so rewarding and fun. But at times it can be challenging, like when a flight is delayed or canceled. Or when you have some bad experience, like the air conditioning not working in your room or getting Montezuma's Revenge. If you come prepared, you'll be all right.

If you have done your homework so that you know what to expect and you bring what you need (documents, money, meds), that's half of it right there. The other half is attitude. You have to be flexible and adaptable when traveling to the other side of the world.

Think of all the great stories you can tell when you get home. Sometimes, what seems like a bad situation can lead to something good. I've met some of the greatest people and had some of the best experiences as a result of a detour or delay.

HEALTH: If you have a health condition, such as heart trouble or diabetes, you should consult your doctor before taking any trip. You also need to check with the authorities to find out if you need a letter from your doctor (if taking injections or narcotics) and there are airline rules about carrying oxygen and some types of inhalers.

Be sure you talk to your doctor before getting any vaccinations to make sure they won't interfere with any meds you're on. I have heard of people suffering from mild hallucinations while on anti-malaria medication and certain motion sickness drugs. I have taken both and never had any adverse reactions, but you should discuss this with your doctor or pharmacist, who probably knows more about side effects than your doctor.

MONEY: Make sure you have enough in the right denomination. I recommend the 1/3 system, which is 1/3 cash in small bills and 1/3 credit card (two different ones) and 1/3 traveler's cheques. You don't have to do this; it's just a recommendation based on my experience. You may get somewhere that doesn't take credit cards. It happens more than you think in foreign countries, especially developing countries. Traveler's cheques are in case your wallet or bag gets stolen; you can replace those, so you're not out the money.

You need to authorize your credit card company to approve

overseas transactions as most will block them now due to credit card/identity theft. Even then, you may find they have 'frozen activity' on your account. That's why I recommend a backup credit card. Check the transaction fees and rates (and balances and rewards) before deciding which card to take.

You can even opt for a pre-paid travel credit card. Both Visa and MasterCard are widely accepted, but Discover and American Express are not as widely accepted.

You can exchange cash at exchange bureaus at the airport or a bank or even your hotel. Make sure you do that before you leave for a less populated or remote destination on your trip. While on safari, most lodges will charge purchases to your room. They don't take foreign currency or traveler's cheques. They will, however, accept credit cards.

Keep your contact information separate from your traveler's cheques and credit cards. If they get stolen, you will have the information you need to replace the traveler's cheques and cancel the credit cards. You don't want to wait until you get home to do that as it will be too late by that time.

In many safari camps, cash is not accepted unless it is the local currency. However, you can pay by credit card or charge optional items to your room. Be advised that your credit card company may charge a foreign transaction fee.

* * *

What to Pack...

Even if it is not the rainy season, you may still experience a downpour or muddy trails when on a gorilla trek or walking safari. Always wear long pants to protect your legs and always bring a rain jacket.

Waterproof hiking boots and good **socks** that wick moisture

Gators (I'm not talking about garden boots or waders. Gators are waterproof sleeves that goes over part of your boot and pant leg. This water-resistant sleeve keeps water out if it is raining or when you are crossing a creek. It also keeps insects out, including mosquitos and ants. But speaking of gators, don't bring rubber boots. While they are good for gardening and short walks in the rain, they are not good for long, difficult treks in mountainous terrain.

Cooling towel (optional)

Waterproof backpack (Some call this a daypack. While it should be lightweight, it also needs to be big enough to hold your lunch, water bottles/thermos, jacket, and personal items)

***raincoat** and **waterproof jacket/coat** (depending on season)

***hat/visor/cap**

***gloves and scarf** (depending on season)

***garden gloves** (if going on a gorilla trek, gloves are good protection against nettles)

***sunscreen** (30 SPF)

***insect repellent** (should contain at least 30% DEET)

***bathing suit and cover-up**

***shower shoes/sandals** (for bathing, swimming, and spa visits).

***nice outfit**, such as a long, black skirt and dressy blouse with suitable shoes (optional, unless your itinerary includes a special welcome party or such)

***casual clothes** (2 pants, 2 shorts, 3 short and 3 long t-shirts)

***undergarments**

***sleeping attire**

***alarm clock**

***watch** (don't pack jewelry except for costume jewelry; be careful if your watch is not waterproof)

***toiletries, comb/hairbrush, glasses/contact lenses/sunglasses**

***book or tablet/reader** (optional)

***cell phone** (optional)

***travel documents**

***cash/credit cards/travelers cheques** (optional)

***chargers and extra batteries** for iPod, phones, cameras, etc.

***prescription medications** (be sure to keep pills in prescription bottles, and you may need a doctor's note if you are carrying needles for diabetes meds or inhalers for asthma)

*over the counter meds (such as aspirin, seasickness pills, antacids, bandages, and topical ointment, such as Neosporin®)

*converters and adaptors if you have an electric razor, curling iron, mobile phone/tablet, hair dryer (most hotels and lodges have hair dryers but self-catering camps will not) or if you think you'll need to charge your camera batteries or will have some medical equipment that requires an outlet.

Note: 220/230 V; Plug M. I recommend investing in a universal adapter and converter kit. You'll have what you need wherever you go. You must have a converter as well as an adapter.

Be sure to pack the right clothes. If it is winter (remember their seasons are opposite) when you visit, be sure to pack heavier pants, a coat, gloves and scarf. If it is summer there when you visit, be sure to pack lightweight, comfortable clothes.

If you're planning on doing any special interest activities, be sure to pack what you need for that, such as a prescription mask if going snorkeling or shark diving. All companies provide wetsuits and masks but not prescription masks. Usually, walking sticks are available at no cost at your lodge for the gorilla treks.

Be aware that internal flights in Africa have strict weight limits. But there is no need to pack a lot of clothes. Most lodges, hotels, and camps have laundry service. Wear hiking boots and jacket on board, and you have removed your heaviest (and bulkiest) items from your checked bag.

TERRANCE ZEPKE

FYI: Be sure to check for the latest updates from TSA so that you know what you can and can't take on the plane in your carry-on bag or pack in your suitcase. Also, you should check with your airline regarding their latest baggage restrictions (and baggage fees). There are weight limits and size limitations for both carry-on bags and checked luggage, which varies according to the airline. Certain items are banned or restricted to three ounces or less and limited to certain types of containers, as determined by TSA.

These restrictions are subject to change periodically. http://www.tsa.gov/traveler-information/packing-tip

* * *

FYI: You can schedule a stopover on route home. Depending on the airline you use, you could spend a day or two in Istanbul, Turkey, London, England; Amsterdam, Holland; Nairobi, Kenya: Brussels, Belgium; or Paris, France. There are many possible routes, so you need to consider this option while you are still in the planning stages.

* * *

Resources

Here are a few recommendations:

Dian Fossey Gorilla Fund International (Adopt a gorilla!)
https://gorillafund.org/

African Wildlife Foundation Gorilla Page
http://www.awf.org/wildlife-conservation/mountain-gorilla

National Geographic Mountain Gorilla Page
https://www.nationalgeographic.com/animals/mammals/m/mountain-gorilla/

List of tour operators in Uganda
https://www.safaribookings.com/operators/uganda and
http://www.bwindiforestnationalpark.com/gorilla-safari-companies.html

List of tour operators in Rwanda
https://www.safaribookings.com/tours/rwanda

For a list of U.S. **travel agents** specializing in East Africa trips, check out the American Society of Travel Agents, http://www.asta.org/. There are several reputable tour companies who offer gorilla safaris, such as International Expeditions, Natural Habitat, and Goway.

Official Uganda Tourism Board
http://visituganda.com/

Official Rwanda Tourism Board
https://rwanda-tourism.com/ and
http://www.aboutrwanda.com/rwanda-tour-operators/

As promised, here's the link to the interview I did on *Terrance Talks Travel: Über Adventures* with a gal who had a serious medical condition but participated in a strenuous Rwanda gorilla safari as part of an around the world adventure she planned before her surgery. She shares her incredible and inspiring story: http://terrancetalkstravel.com/uber-adventures-traveling-with-a-serious-medical-condition/

Safari Resources

FYI: On Safari, there is a term, Big Five, which is what most tourists want to see. These five mammals include the African elephant, Rhinoceros, African buffalo, Lion, and Leopard.

You can see all kinds of other wonderful animals (according to the region). You may wish to create a safari animal checklist or use one of these handy apps while on safari:

African-Safari Wildlife Guide can be downloaded before leaving home so that no Internet connection is needed. iPhone & iPad. $.
https://itunes.apple.com/us/app/id341885050?mt=8

The Kingdon Guide to African Mammals includes close to 500 species. iPhone, iPod touch & iPad. $.
https://itunes.apple.com/us/app/id336901877?mt=8

Audubon African Wildlife includes mammals, birds, and reptiles. iPhone & iPad. $.
https://itunes.apple.com/us/app/id378562356?mt=8

Africa: Live app is my favorite. It offers real-time safari sightings with live maps and interactive markers, plus live social media streams and the ability to add sightings and upload photos. Android and Apple Smartphones. FREE.
https://itunes.apple.com/us/app/id552879842?mt=8

TERRANCE TALKS TRAVEL: A
POCKET GUIDE TO EAST AFRICA'S
UGANDA & RWANDA

Guides are well-trained to know all the animals so they will quickly identify any and all animals you spot while on safari. However, if there is a bird or reptile they don't recognize, they have wildlife encyclopedias and will quickly find the answer for you.

* * *

Special Dates & Events

The following is a list of public holidays:

New Year's Day (1/1)
Day After **New Year's Day** (1/2) Rwanda only
Liberation Day (1/26)
Heroes Day (2/1) Rwanda only
Archbishop Janani Luwum Day (2/16)
Womens Day (3/8)
Good Friday, Easter, & Easter Monday (March/April)
Tutsi Genocide Memorial Day (4/7) Rwanda only
Labor Day (5/1)
Martry's Day (6/1)
Heroes Day (6/9) Uganda only
Eid-al-Fitr (6/15)
Liberation Day (7/4) Rwanda only
Umuganura Day (8/3) Rwanda only
Assumption of Mary (8/15) Rwanda only
Eid-al-Adha (8/22)

Independence Day (10/9)
Christmas Day (12/25)
Boxing Day (12/26)

Observances: March Equinox (3/20), June Solstice (6/21), September Equinox (9/23), and December Solstice (12/21).

* * *

This is a list of major annual events throughout Uganda and Rwanda:

Rwanda Mini Film Festival (March) is a forum for amateur film makers to showcase their work. It is open to everyone from students to professionals so long as they adhere to the festival's entry requirements. (Rwanda).

Gorilla Naming Ceremony (June) is when baby gorillas are named by park guides. There is a ceremony with music and traditional dance. (Rwanda).

Hillywood Film Festival (July) showcases Rwanda's film industry. Filmmakers across Africa participate, and there are also workshops and talks, in addition to film screenings.

Centre X Centre Festival (August) celebrates Rwandan theater. The theme changes from year to year but relates to the message of "Arts and Peace." (Rwanda).

Festival on the Nile (August) features music, dance, storytelling, food, dance workshops, children's activities, a parade, and more. It is a celebration of all the cultures (tribes) that live in this area. (Uganda).

Amakula Kampala International Film Festival (September – November) originated in 2004 and has been growing with every passing year. Both new and old films are featured as long as they meet the festival's requirements. (Uganda).

Bayimba International Festival of Music and Arts (September) focuses on the arts and culture of Uganda. Dance, music, film, theater, and visual arts are all featured in this popular three-day festival held in the Uganda National Theatre in Kampala. (Uganda).

B-Global Indigenous Hip Hop Festival (September) is a four-day festival celebrating Uganda's unique twist on hip hop. It is meant to celebrate this musical style and promote peace and harmony. (Uganda).

KigaliUp! Rwandan Music Festival (September) is a huge outdoor music festival. Held in Kigali, the event features artists from all genres, including R&B, Rwandan Pop, and traditional folk music. (Rwanda).

Festival Arts Azimuts (October) is commonly referred to as FAAZ. It brings together visual artists, dancers, and musicians. In addition to great performances, well-known speakers inspire participants with their stories. (Rwanda).

Nile Gold Jazz Safari (October) is a chance to hear some of the greatest jazz musicians in the world. (Uganda).

This Is Uganda (December) is about showcasing Uganda's art, music, poetry, and dance. The focus is on female performers and artists because the event is meant to promote women's rights and education. (Uganda).

* * *

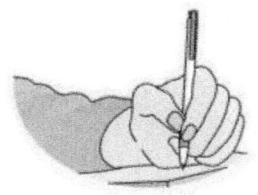

Fun Quiz

1. What is the only country in Africa that is home to tree-climbing lions?
   a. Rwanda
   b. Uganda
   c. Botswana
   d. Tanzania

2. How many mountain gorillas are there?
   a. Less than 1,000
   b. Less than 100
   c. More than 1,000
   d. There is no such thing as a mountain gorilla.

3. The largest lake in Africa is Lake Victoria. It is in what country?
    a. Uganda, Rwanda & Kenya
    b. Rwanda & Tanzania
    c. Uganda, Kenya & Tanzania
    d. Rwanda

4. What is the largest mountain range in Africa?
    a. Mount Kilimanjaro
    b. Virunga
    c. Rwenzori
    d. Dranesburk

5. What is the biggest export of Rwanda?
    a. Lemons
    b. Tea
    c. Coffee
    d. Diamonds

6. What is the biggest export of Uganda?
a. Lemons
b. Tea
c. Coffee
d. Diamonds

7. Children under 18 make up more than half of Uganda's population. True or False?
   a. True
   b. False

8. What is the most commonly seen animal on an East African safari?
   a. Black rhinos
   b. Cheetahs
   c. Chimpanzees
   d. Lions

9. What is the least commonly seen animal on an East African safari?
   a. Lions
   b. Black rhinos
   c. Cheetahs
   d. Tigers

10. Who was involved in Rwanda's horrific Genocide War?
    a. Batwa and Hutu
    b. Bawa and Tutsi
    c. Tutsi and Maasai
    d. Hutu and Tutsi

* * *

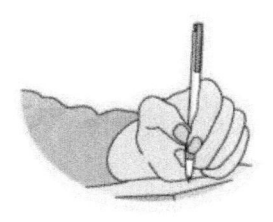

East Africa Quiz Answers

1. b (While all lions can climb trees, most do not, except in one place in Uganda where they can be seen certain times of day lounging in trees).
2. a (There are 600-800 mountain gorillas still in existence).
3. c
4. c (While Mount Kilimanjaro is the highest peak in Africa, **Rwenzori** is the *highest* mountain range in Africa. It forms the border between Uganda and the DRC).
5. b (Tea is the #1 export at more than 15,000 tons per year, but coffee is a close second).
6. c
7. a

8. d
9. c (Cheetahs are rarely seen. Tigers are only in Asia and Black rhinos are on the brink of extinction).
10. d

Black Rhinos

* * *

TERRANCE ZEPKE

A Picture Is Worth

A Thousand Words…

Aaahhhhhhhhhh!

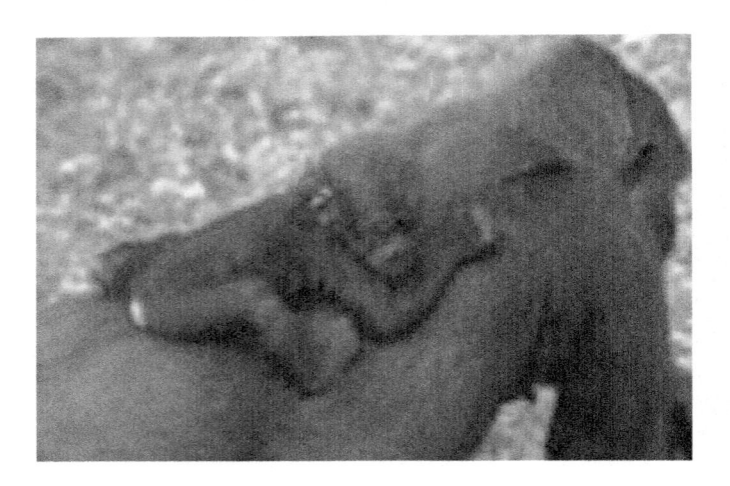

Break time in the bush...nice!

Me and our guide/driver, Joseph, crossing the Equator.

African women are amazing. They can carry anything on their heads, including large logs!

I was so happy to get this photo as it's unusual to see hippos out of the water and even more rare to catch them sleeping.

TERRANCE ZEPKE

Double trouble!

Chimpanzee

TERRANCE ZEPKE

One of many waterfalls we saw in Bwindi Impenetrable Forest

TERRANCE TALKS TRAVEL: A
POCKET GUIDE TO EAST AFRICA'S
UGANDA & RWANDA

View from our balcony at Bwindi & our room

Ugandan beer tastes so good after a long safari day.

Upon landing at the small airstrip, safari guides are waiting to whisk travelers off to camp to begin their safari adventure.

TERRANCE ZEPKE

You often dine al fresco at safari camps.

Malawi Lodge Lounge…not bad, huh?

TERRANCE ZEPKE

Hot air balloon safaris and boat safaris are fun options.

TERRANCE TALKS TRAVEL: A
POCKET GUIDE TO EAST AFRICA'S
UGANDA & RWANDA

African Elephant and Striped Hyena

There is nothing like breakfast in the bush, which included omelets and Belgium waffles (and they even set up a porta potty!)

Queen Elizabeth National Park is one of the few places where you will find tree-climbing lions. The lions love to nap in fig trees.

TERRANCE ZEPKE

The Batwa are an indigenous tribe who once lived in Bwindi Forest.

TERRANCE TALKS TRAVEL: A
POCKET GUIDE TO EAST AFRICA'S
UGANDA & RWANDA

TERRANCE ZEPKE

Close up of Silverback Gorilla & a Gorilla hand.

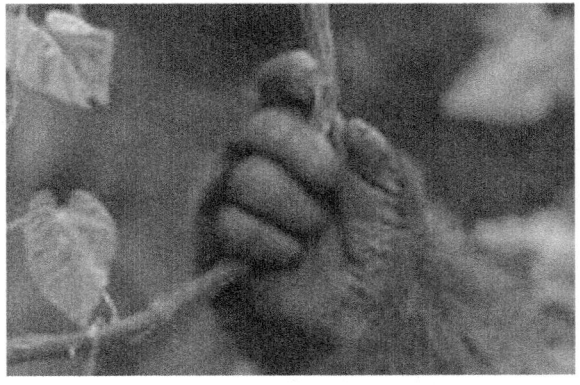

TERRANCE TALKSTRAVEL: A
POCKET GUIDE TO EAST AFRICA'S
UGANDA & RWANDA

Male Silverbacks can weigh up to 600 pounds. They must be big and strong to protect their troop.

TERRANCE ZEPKE

I got close to some gorillas!

Greatest day ever!

Warthogs and storks

Some of the gorilla trek was very challenging. I am mindful that it is a long way down that mountain if I slip and fall!

The Congo

TERRANCE ZEPKE

Some animals we saw include the Topi and Pelicans.

TERRANCE TALKS TRAVEL: A
POCKET GUIDE TO EAST AFRICA'S
UGANDA & RWANDA

Spiny Tree

TERRANCE ZEPKE

Colobus Monkey

TERRANCE TALKS TRAVEL: A
POCKET GUIDE TO EAST AFRICA'S
UGANDA & RWANDA

Baboons are hard to photograph as they are fast and mean. You can't get near them or let them near you as they may attack or steal your stuff!

**Harvesting Tea
(Tea and coffee are the main exports of
Uganda).**

TERRANCE TALKS TRAVEL: A
POCKET GUIDE TO EAST AFRICA'S
UGANDA & RWANDA

Gorillas spend half the day eating.

TERRANCE ZEPKE

The people are so friendly, especially the kids.

BONUS!

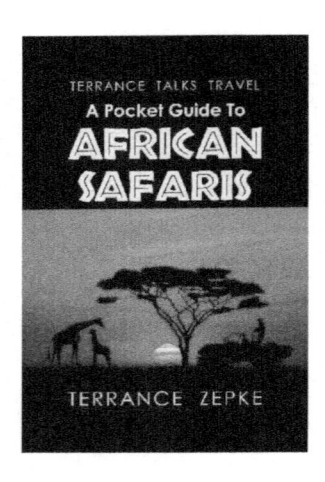

Sneak Peek of

TERRANCE TALKS TRAVEL:

A Pocket Guide to African Safaris

TERRANCE ZEPKE

CONTENTS

Introduction
Fun Facts
Ten Steps to Planning A Perfect Safari
    Step #1: Decide Where & How To Go
    Step #2: Best Time To Go
    Step #3: How To Get The Best Price
    Step #4: Book Your Safari
    Step #5: Find A Flight
    Step #6: Buy Travel Insurance
    Step #7: Vaccinations
    Step #8: Visas & Passports
    Step #9: What To Pack
    Step #10: Get Psyched
Safari Animals Checklist
List of Safari Companies & Safari Cruises
Titles by Terrance
Pix & Notes
Index

Step #3: How to Get the Best Price

Perhaps this should be the first chapter of this reference as this is always one of the biggest concerns and considerations of any trip. Safaris are not as expensive as you think, especially if you know what you're doing. Here are five ways to save lots of money and get the best price possible on any safari:

1. Everything I've read from other travel experts tells safari participants to go in the off-season to save money. Since this is the rainy season, I don't like to give that advice. You can get really good deals (up to 40% off) and get lucky with decent weather. But you can also be unlucky with the weather, and this is no fun on safari. There are three travel seasons: low, high, and off. As I have just mentioned, off-season means worst time to go, so this is when the lowest prices are offered. High season means peak season or best time to go, so expect the highest prices during this time. Traveling in the low season can be a happy compromise. **I recommend going on safari during the low season as the rainy season will be over but the high season has not yet**

kicked in. See Step #2 for specific information.

2. **Avoid the most expensive places, such as Botswana, Namibia, Madagascar, Uganda, and Rwanda**. If there are animals there you want to see; such as gorillas or lemurs, you will have to go to these places and will pay a premium price. However, using the resources and strategies included in this reference (including air consolidators and budget operators) will still save you money.

   A great safari destination that is a big bargain is the **Republic of Malawi** - formerly known as Nyasaland - is a landlocked country bordered by Zambia to the northwest, Tanzania to the northeast, and Mozambique to the east, west, and south. The country gets its name from Maravi, which is one of the original Bantu tribes that inhabited the region. Malawi's climate is hot in the low lying southern areas and temperate in the northern highlands. Its official languages are English and Chichewa, and the capital city is Lilongwe.

The country is divided into three regions; the Northern, Central, and Southern. The Northern region is mountainous, with the highest peaks reaching over 8,200 feet. It also has rugged escarpments, valleys, and thickly forested slopes. The Central region is mainly a plateau, over 3,300-feet high, with fine upland scenery. The Southern is mostly low-lying except for the 6,890-foot high Zomba Plateau and isolated

Mulanje Massif in the southeast.

Malawi offers a variety of landscapes, accessible forest reserves, wildlife and activities like water sports, trekking and game viewing in the most natural settings. In short, a trip to Malawi is nothing but a true African experience with a relatively minimal cost. Last year it received Lonely Planet's 'Top Ten Countries' Award.

Lilongwe is known as the Garden City. It is surrounded by colorful flowering trees that complement its modern architecture and parklands. The old town is built around the former village of Lilongwe, while the new town has modern commercial structures. Blantyre Mission, Mandela House, March 3 House, Chichiri

Museum and the National Museum of Malawi are some of the places you can visit in Blantyre.

Great Rift Valley is one of the most spectacular sights in the country. Michiru Mountain Conservation, Fisherman's Rest, and the Lilongwe Nature Sanctuary are some of the various, breathtaking nature parks to visit. You can also check out Lake Malawi, which is the third largest lake in Africa. If you plan to visit an area near the countryside, you should have a guide with you at all times.

In addition to safaris, fishing, snorkeling, scuba diving, bird watching, swimming, and village visits are offered. For a list of accommodations, activities, safaris, and more, visit http://www.malawitourism.com/

3. **Don't stay at luxury lodges and camps** ($$$$). Instead, pick moderate lodges or camps ($$$). Or better still, try full-service mobile camping. Guests enjoy walk-in dome tents, raised cots, wash basins, a flush toilet (this will be in a separate tent), hot-water bucket showers, and a dining tent (meals will be cooked over the campfire and served by the camp staff). As you can tell, this is not exactly roughing it! Or another option is participatory "overland" camping where participants load their own luggage, help set up camp, and lend a hand preparing meals. A true safari!

4. **Look at the bottom line**. What is included? Tips, meals, taxes, and extensions can add

up. You may find that a more expensive safari was the better price once all the figures were tallied up. Also, scale back on add-ons if you're watching the bottom line. Carefully pick and choose your indulgences. For example, opt for the hot-air balloon safari and skip the visit to Sun City's crocodile sanctuary or vice versa.

5. **Sign up to be notified about specials offered by airlines and safari companies. Use budget operators** (see list provided in the back of this reference) to get best deals, as well as **iSafari**, a handy online safari planning tool. If you're working with a travel agent, be sure to let her know your budget and what you care most about seeing and doing.
http://isafari.nathab.com/

The 3 "C's":
Cash, Cheques and Credit Cards.

How much money do you need during your trip? That depends on you and your trip. Some people are not comfortable carrying much cash while others find it very reassuring to have a lot of cash with them while traveling in case of an emergency. It also depends on what is included in your package. While some may prefer to charge everything, others try to use their card as little as possible.

Keep in mind while deciding how much cash to bring, that there are things not typically included, such as tipping, laundry, beverages, optional activities, souvenirs, airport visas, taxis, transfers (some lodges charge for pick up and drop off service), and some meals. All meals are usually included in safari camps and lodges but are not typically included in hotels, hostels, and other types of lodging.

How much cash you carry with you depends on your comfort level. Some folks don't like to have much cash on them. Others feel better knowing they are far from home with a wad of cash. For a two-week safari trip, I recommend taking a minimum of $500 in cash. But you should do whatever you are most comfortable doing. If your trip is largely all-inclusive, you may want to take no more than $300. Or it may make you feel more assured to carry $800, especially if you prefer not to use your credit card any more than necessary. Use your credit card for large purchases and save your cash for smaller purchases, such as snacks, tips, and souvenirs.

I recommend the 1/3 system, which is 1/3 cash in small bills, 1/3 credit card (2 different ones), and 1/3 traveler's cheques (or a prepaid credit/debit card).

Note: You need to authorize your credit card company to approve overseas transactions as most will block them now due to identity theft and fraud. The card issuer will ask you for dates and destinations to denote on your account. Even then, you may find they have blocked your card, which means they have frozen all activity on your account. That's why I recommend a second backup credit card. Check the transaction fees and rates (and balances and rewards) before deciding which card to take. You can even opt for a pre-paid travel credit card. That way there is no risk with someone getting hold of the number of a high limit credit card. I recommend sticking to Visa® and MasterCard® as they are widely accepted, whereas Discover, Diner's Card®, and American Express® are not as much so.

It is often hard to access money

while traveling, especially in Africa. ATMs are readily available in South Africa but not in most other countries with a few exceptions.

You can exchange cash at exchange bureaus at the airport or a bank or even your hotel. Make sure you do that before you leave for a remote destination on your trip, such as Victoria Falls. While on safari, most lodges will accept local currency, and you can charge any charges made at the lodge to your room. Typically, they don't take foreign currency or traveler's cheques. They will, however, accept credit cards, at check out.

You can even exchange money before leaving home if you prefer to take care of it before you go. This can be accomplished at a large bank, such as Bank of America, or through a service, such as www.travelexinsurance.com.

You will be required to pay a deposit to reserve the trip. Typically, sixty days before departure, the rest of the balance is due. This date will be on the deposit contract you signed when you booked the trip. Make sure you circle the date the balance is due and put it on your calendar so that your trip doesn't get "released" (canceled) by mistake. A good travel agent or tour operator will remind you, but things do happen.

Step #4: Book Your Safari

Now that you have decided where you want to go and when you want to go, it is time to book your trip. You will find a list of reputable companies at the back of this reference.

If you find a package from a company that is not listed in this book just be sure to do your research. This means reading the fine print. When is the trip? Check to make sure it is not during the wrong season. What is included? What is excluded? Is this company a member of an accredited organization, such as USTOA and ASTA? Do they have any complaints filed against them? Are there are customer reviews on the company's site or feedback on travel sites, such as Yelp and TripAdvisor? How long have they been in business? How long have they been offering this trip? I wouldn't book a trip with a company who just started offering a particular trip, but if they've been running this trip for ten years, chances are they know what they're doing.

You can also put together a package yourself by booking directly with a lodge and booking your flights and transfers. But whatever you do, make sure that you're in good hands and that you understand what you have signed up for.

*   *   *

Step #5: Find a Flight

If international airfare is included in your package, you can skip to Step #6. If you are making your own arrangements, I have included some resources at the end of this section to help you with this step.

Normally, fares to most African cities from the U.S., Canada, and Europe run from $800 - $1,800, depending on the season and your route. That said, I have seen them higher and lower than this from time to time.

The best plan is to use airline miles you have judiciously socked away. It doesn't matter if your airline flies to your African destination or not. Nearly all airlines are in alliances these days, which means that you can fly on any of the airlines that are partners with your airline. Most major airlines are part of Star Alliance or One World.

Take advantage of periodic specials when you can buy so many miles and get up to 100% more at no cost. Pay your bills using a credit card that rewards you with airline miles (and then pay that card off using the money you were going to use to pay your bills). This is where the planning pays off.

If you don't have enough miles, then set up airfare alerts through **Bing, One Travel, BootsnAll Travel, STA Travel**, and **Cheap Tickets**. Do not wait for 'last minute specials' as there aren't any. Seats to Africa fill up without having to offer incentives.

FYI: You can schedule a stopover in Europe and make that a bonus to your safari! Traveling to Africa via Europe opens up lots more options for fliers, such as Paris and Cairo. You can check your favorite travel sites, such as **Kayak, Bing, and Priceline**. Additionally, here are a few good resources for cheap airfares:

www.airlineconsolidator.com
www.cheapoair.com
www.airfarewatchdog.com
www.cheaptickets.com
www.onetravel.com
www.travelzoo.com

* * *

TERRANCE ZEPKE

TERRANCE ZEPKE
Series Reading Order & Guide

Series List

Most Haunted Series

Terrance Talks Travel Series

Cheap Travel Series

Spookiest Series

Stop Talking Series

Carolinas for Kids Series

Ghosts of the Carolinas Series

Books & Guides for the Carolinas Series

& More Books by Terrance Zepke

≈

Introduction

Here is a list of titles by Terrance Zepke. They are presented in chronological order although they do not need to be read in any particular order. Also included is an author bio, a personal message from Terrance, and some other information you may find helpful. All books are available as digital and print books. They can be found on Amazon, Barnes and Noble, Kobo, Apple iBooks, GooglePlay, Smashwords, or through your favorite independent bookseller.

For more about this author and her books visit her Author Page at: http://www.amazon.com/Terrance-Zepke/e/B000APJNIA/.

You can also connect with Terrance on Twitter **@terrancezepke** or on

www.facebook.com/terrancezepke

www.pinterest.com/terrancezepke

TERRANCE TALKS TRAVEL

Podcast

You can follow her travel show, **TERRANCE TALKS TRAVEL: ÜBER ADVENTURES on** **www.blogtalkradio.com/terrancetalkstravel** or subscribe to it at **iTunes.**

Warning: Listening to this show could lead to a spectacular South African safari, hot-air ballooning over the Swiss Alps, Disney Adventures, and Tornado Tours!

TERRANCE ZEPKE

≈

Terrance Zepke is co-host of the writing show, **A WRITER'S JOURNEY: FROM BLANK PAGE TO PUBLISHED.** All episodes can be found on **iTunes** or on **www.terrancezepke.com**.

≈

AUTHOR BIO

Terrance Zepke studied Journalism at the University of Tennessee and later received a Master's degree in Mass Communications from the University of South Carolina. She studied parapsychology at the renowned Rhine Research Center.

Zepke spends much of her time happily traveling around the world but always returns home to the Carolinas where she lives part-time in both states. She has written hundreds of articles and more than fifty books. She is the host of *Terrance Talks Travel: Über Adventures* and co-host of *A Writer's Journey: From Blank Page to Published*. Additionally, this award-winning and best-selling author has been featured in many publications and programs, such as NPR, CNN, *The Washington Post,* Associated Press, Travel with Rick Steves, Around the World, *Publishers Weekly,* World Travel & Dining with Pierre Wolfe, *San Francisco Chronicle*, Good Morning Show, *Detroit Free*

Press, The Learning Channel, and The Travel Channel.

When she's not investigating haunted places, searching for pirate treasure, or climbing lighthouses, she is most likely packing for her next adventure to some far flung place, such as Reykjavik or Kwazulu Natal. Some of her favorite adventures include piranha fishing on the Amazon, shark cage diving in South Africa, hiking the Andes Mountains Inca Trail, camping in the Himalayas, dog-sledding in the Arctic Circle, and a gorilla safari in the Congo.

≈

MOST HAUNTED SERIES

A Ghost Hunter's Guide to the Most Haunted Places in America (2012)
https://read.amazon.com/kp/embed?asin=B0085SG22O&preview=newtab&linkCode=kpe&ref_=cm_sw_r_kb_dp_zerQwb1AMJ0R4

A Ghost Hunter's Guide to the Most Haunted Houses in America (2013)
https://read.amazon.com/kp/embed?asin=B00C3PUMGC&preview=newtab&linkCode=kpe&ref_=cm_sw_r_kb_dp_BfrQwb1WF1Y6T

A Ghost Hunter's Guide to the Most Haunted Hotels & Inns in America (2014)
https://read.amazon.com/kp/embed?asin=B00C3PUMGC&preview=newtab&linkCode=kpe

A Ghost Hunter's Guide to the Most Haunted Historic Sites in America (2016)
https://www.amazon.com/Ghost-Hunters-Haunted-Historic-America-ebook/dp/B01LXADK90/ref=sr_1_1?s=books&ie=UTF8&qid=1475973918&sr=1-1&keywords=a+ghost+hunter%27s+guide+to+the+most+haunted+historic+sites+in+america

TERRANCE ZEPKE

The Ghost Hunter's MOST HAUNTED Box Set (3 in 1): Discover America's Most Haunted Destinations (2016)
https://read.amazon.com/kp/embed?asin=B01HISAAJM&preview=newtab&linkCode=kpe&ref_=cm_sw_r_kb_dp_ulz-xbNKND7VT

MOST HAUNTED and SPOOKIEST Sampler Box Set: Featuring *A GHOST HUNTER'S GUIDE TO THE MOST HAUNTED PLACES IN AMERICA* and *SPOOKIEST CEMETERIES* (2017)
https://read.amazon.com/kp/embed?asin=B01N17EEOM&preview=newtab&linkCode=kpe&ref_=cm_sw_r_kb_dp_.JFLybCTN3QEF

A Ghost Hunter's Guide to the Most Haunted Places in the World (2018)
https://read.amazon.com/kp/embed?asin=B078ZL382D&preview=newtab&linkCode=kpe&ref_=cm_sw_r_kb_dp_s55IAb5MYWXSG

≈

TERRANCE TALKS TRAVEL SERIES

Terrance Talks Travel: A Pocket Guide to South Africa (2015)
https://read.amazon.com/kp/embed?asin=B0
0PSTFTLI&preview=newtab&linkCode=kp
e&ref_=cm_sw_r_kb_dp_pirQwb12XZX65

Terrance Talks Travel: A Pocket Guide to African Safaris (2015)
https://read.amazon.com/kp/embed?asin=B0
0PSTFZSA&preview=newtab&linkCode=k
pe&ref_=cm_sw_r_kb_dp_jhrQwb0P8Z87
G

Terrance Talks Travel: A Pocket Guide to Adventure Travel (2015)
https://read.amazon.com/kp/embed?asin=B0
0UKMAVQG&preview=newtab&linkCode
=kpe&ref_=cm_sw_r_kb_dp_ThrQwb1PV
VZAZ

Terrance Talks Travel: A Pocket Guide to Florida Keys (including Key West & The Everglades) (2016)
http://www.amazon.com/Terrance-Talks-

TERRANCE ZEPKE

Travel-Including-Everglades-ebook/dp/B01EWHML58/ref=sr_1_1?s=books&ie=UTF8&qid=1461897775&sr=1-1&keywords=terrance+talks+travel%3A+a+pocket+guide+to+the+florida+keys

Terrance Talks Travel: The Quirky Tourist Guide to Key West (2017)
https://www.amazon.com/Terrance-Zepke/e/B000APJNIA/ref=sr_ntt_srch_lnk_1?qid=1485052308&sr=8-1

Terrance Talks Travel: The Quirky Tourist Guide to Cape Town (2017)
https://www.amazon.com/Terrance-Zepke/e/B000APJNIA/ref=sr_ntt_srch_lnk_1?qid=1485052308&sr=8-1

Terrance Talks Travel: The Quirky Tourist Guide to Reykjavik (2017)
https://www.amazon.com/Terrance-Zepke/e/B000APJNIA/ref=sr_ntt_srch_lnk_15?qid=1488514258&sr=8-15

Terrance Talks Travel: The Quirky Tourist Guide to Charleston, South Carolina (2017)
https://www.amazon.com/Terrance-Zepke/e/B000APJNIA/ref=sr_ntt_srch_lnk_15?qid=1488514258&sr=8-15

Terrance Talks Travel: The Quirky Tourist Guide to Ushuaia (2017)
https://www.amazon.com/Terrance-Zepke/e/B000APJNIA/ref=sr_ntt_srch_lnk_15?qid=1488514258&sr=8-15

Terrance Talks Travel: The Quirky Tourist Guide to Antarctica (2017)
https://www.amazon.com/Terrance-Zepke/e/B000APJNIA/ref=sr_ntt_srch_lnk_1?qid=1489092624&sr=8-1

TERRANCE TALKS TRAVEL: The Quirky Tourist Guide to Machu Picchu & Cuzco (Peru) 2017
https://read.amazon.com/kp/embed?asin=B07147HLQY&preview=newtab&linkCode=kpe&ref_=cm_sw_r_kb_dp_HmZmzb9FT5E0P

African Safari Box Set: Featuring TERRANCE TALKS TRAVEL: A Pocket Guide to South Africa and TERRANCE TALKS TRAVEL: A Pocket Guide to African Safaris (2017)
https://read.amazon.com/kp/embed?asin=B01MUH6VJU&preview=newtab&linkCode=kpe&ref_=cm_sw_r_kb_dp_xLFLybAQKFA0B

TERRANCE ZEPKE

Terrance Talks Travel: A Pocket Guide to East Africa's Uganda and Rwanda (2018)
https://www.amazon.com/Terrance-Zepke/e/B000APJNIA/ref=dp_byline_cont_ebooks_1

≈

CHEAP TRAVEL SERIES

How to Cruise Cheap! (2017)
https://www.amazon.com/Cruise-Cheap-CHEAP-TRAVEL-Book-ebook/dp/B01N6NYM1N/

How to Fly Cheap! (2017)
https://www.amazon.com/How-Cheap-CHEAP-TRAVEL-Book-ebook/dp/B01N7Q81YG/

How to Travel Cheap! (2017)
https://read.amazon.com/kp/embed?asin=B01N7Q81YG&preview=newtab&linkCode=kpe&ref_=cm_sw_r_kb_dp_j78KybJVSCXDX

How to Travel FREE or Get Paid to Travel! (2017)
https://read.amazon.com/kp/embed?asin=B01N7Q81YG&preview=newtab&linkCode=kpe&ref_=cm_sw_r_kb_dp_j78KybJVSCXDX

CHEAP TRAVEL SERIES (4 IN 1) BOX SET (2017)
https://read.amazon.com/kp/embed?asin=B071ZGV1TY&preview=newtab&linkCode=kpe&ref_=cm_sw_r_kb_dp_-f1JAb8Y7SJHD

TERRANCE ZEPKE

SPOOKIEST SERIES

Spookiest Lighthouses (2013)
https://read.amazon.com/kp/embed?asin=B0
0EAAQA2S&preview

Spookiest Battlefields (2015)
https://read.amazon.com/kp/embed?asin=B0
0XUSWS3G&preview=newtab&linkCode=
kpe&ref_=cm_sw_r_kb_dp_okrQwb0TR9F
8M

Spookiest Cemeteries (2016)
http://www.amazon.com/Terrance-
Zepke/e/B000APJNIA/ref=sr_ntt_srch_lnk_
1?qid=1457641303&sr=8-1

Spookiest Objects (2017)
https://read.amazon.com/kp/embed?asin=B0
728FMVZF&preview=newtab&linkCode=k
pe&ref_=cm_sw_r_kb_dp_eqZmzbN2172V
R

*Spookiest Box Set (3 in 1): Discover
America's Most Haunted Destinations*
(2016)
https://read.amazon.com/kp/embed?asin=B0
1HH2OM4I&preview=newtab&linkCode=k
pe&ref_=cm_sw_r_kb_dp_Anz-
xbT3SDEZS

MOST HAUNTED and SPOOKIEST Sampler Box Set: Featuring *A GHOST HUNTER'S GUIDE TO THE MOST HAUNTED PLACES IN AMERICA* and *SPOOKIEST CEMETERIES* (2017)

https://read.amazon.com/kp/embed?asin=B01N17EEOM&preview=newtab&linkCode=kpe&ref_=cm_sw_r_kb_dp_.JFLybCTN3QEF

≈

TERRANCE ZEPKE

STOP TALKING SERIES

Stop Talking & Start Writing Your Book
(2015)
https://read.amazon.com/kp/embed?asin=B0
12YHTIAY&preview=newtab&linkCode=k
pe&ref_=cm_sw_r_kb_dp_qlrQwb1N7G3Y
F

Stop Talking & Start Publishing Your Book
(2015)
https://read.amazon.com/kp/embed?asin=B0
13HHV1LE&preview=newtab&linkCode=k
pe&ref_=cm_sw_r_kb_dp_WlrQwb1F63M
FD

Stop Talking & Start Selling Your Book
(2015)
https://read.amazon.com/kp/embed?asin=B015Y
AO33K&preview=newtab&linkCode=kpe&ref_
=cm_sw_r_kb_dp_ZkrQwb188J8BE

Stop Talking & Start Writing Your Book
Series (3 in 1) Box Set (2016)
https://www.amazon.com/Stop-Talking-Start-
Writing-Box-
ebook/dp/B01M58J5AZ/ref=sr_1_5?s=books&i
e=UTF8&qid=1475974073&sr=1-
5&keywords=stop+talking+and+start+writing

≈

CAROLINAS FOR KIDS SERIES

Lighthouses of the Carolinas for Kids (2009)
http://www.amazon.com/Lighthouses-Carolinas-Kids-Terrance-Zepke/dp/1561644293/ref=asap_bc?ie=UTF8

Pirates of the Carolinas for Kids (2009)
https://read.amazon.com/kp/embed?asin=B01BJ3VSWK&preview=newtab&linkCode=kpe&ref_=cm_sw_r_kb_dp_rGrXwb0XDTSTA

Ghosts of the Carolinas for Kids (2011)
https://read.amazon.com/kp/embed?asin=B01BJ3VSVQ&preview=newtab&linkCode=kpe&ref_=cm_sw_r_kb_dp_XLrXwb0E7N1AK

≈

TERRANCE ZEPKE

GHOSTS OF THE CAROLINAS SERIES

Ghosts of the Carolina Coasts (1999)
http://www.amazon.com/Ghosts-Carolina-Coasts-Terrance-Zepke/dp/1561641758/ref=asap_bc?ie=UTF8

The Best Ghost Tales of South Carolina (2004)
http://www.amazon.com/Best-Ghost-Tales-South-Carolina/dp/1561643068/ref=asap_bc?ie=UTF8

Ghosts & Legends of the Carolina Coasts (2005)
https://read.amazon.com/kp/embed?asin=B01AGQJABW&preview=newtab&linkCode=kpe&ref_=cm_sw_r_kb_dp_VKrXwb1Q09794

The Best Ghost Tales of North Carolina (2006)
https://read.amazon.com/kp/embed?asin=B01BJ3VSV6&preview=newtab&linkCode=kpe&ref_=cm_sw_r_kb_dp_6IrXwb0XKT90Q

≈

BOOKS & GUIDES FOR THE CAROLINAS SERIES

Pirates of the Carolinas (2005)
http://www.amazon.com/Pirates-Carolinas-Terrance-Zepke/dp/1561643440/ref=asap_bc?ie=UTF8

Coastal South Carolina: Welcome to the Lowcountry (2006)
http://www.amazon.com/Coastal-South-Carolina-Welcome-Lowcountry/dp/1561643483/ref=asap_bc?ie=UTF8

Coastal North Carolina: Its Enchanting Islands, Towns & Communities (2011)
http://www.amazon.com/Coastal-North-Carolina-Terrance-Zepke/dp/1561645117/ref=asap_bc?ie=UTF8

Lighthouses of the Carolinas: A Short History & Guide (2011)
https://read.amazon.com/kp/embed?asin=B01AGQJA7G&preview=newtab&linkCode=kpe&ref_=cm_sw_r_kb_dp_UHrXwb09A22P1

≈

MORE BOOKS BY TERRANCE ZEPKE

Lowcountry Voodoo: Tales, Spells & Boo Hags (2009)
https://read.amazon.com/kp/embed?asin=B018WAGUC6&preview=newtab&linkCode=kpe&ref_=cm_sw_r_kb_dp_UmrQwb19AVSYG

The Encyclopedia of Cheap Travel: Save Up to 90% on Lodging, Flights, Tours, Cruises & More! (2011)
https://read.amazon.com/kp/embed?asin=B005WKGNKY&preview=newtab&linkCode=kpe&ref_=cm_sw_r_kb_dp_InrQwb18QTWGS

Ghosts of Savannah (2012)
http://www.amazon.com/Ghosts-Savannah-Terrance-Zepke/dp/1561645303/ref=asap_bc?ie=UTF8

How to Train Any Puppy or Dog Using Three Simple Strategies (2017)
https://www.amazon.com/Train-Puppy-Using-Simple-Strategies-ebook/dp/B01MZ5GN2M/ref=asap_bc?ie=UTF8

*Fiction books written under a pseudonym

≈

Message from the Author

The primary purpose of this guide is to introduce you to some titles you may not have known about. Another reason for it is to let you know all the ways you can connect with me. Authors love to hear from readers. We truly appreciate you more than you'll ever know. Please feel free to send me a comment or question via the comment form found on every page on www.terrancezepke.com and www.terrancetalkstravel.com If you'd like to learn more about any of my books, you can find in-depth descriptions and "look inside" options through most online booksellers. Also, please note that links to book previews have been included in SERIES section of this booklet for your convenience.

Thank you for your interest and HAPPY READING!

Terrance

TERRANCE ZEPKE

Notes

Notes

TERRANCE ZEPKE

Notes

Index

A

adventure, 11
African Wildlife Foundation, 116, 143
Agathe Uwilingiyimana, 66
airfare, 23
airline rules. *See* TSA
Akagera National Park, 112
American Society of Travel Agents, 144
Angola, 29
annual events, 151
Artisans Market, 113
Arusha Peace Accord, 66

B

Batwa, 96, 160, 181
Belgium, 58, 63, 142, 179
Benedicto Kiwanuka, 83
Best Time to Visit 17, 18
Bing, 215
boda-bodas, 89
bonobo, 34, 35
BootsnAll Travel, 215
Botswana, 201
Britain, 81, 82, 85
Budget, 23
Buganda, 81, 82
Buhoma Lodge, 56
Burundi, 63, 64, 66

Bwindi, 42, *See* Bwindi Impenetrable Forest
Bwindi Impenetrable Forest, 3, 19, 52, 55, 87, 91, 97, 171

C

Cameroon, 28
camping, 205
Cape Town, 3, 5, 159
Central African Republic, 29
cheap airfares, 216
chimpanzee, 24, 34, 97, 99, 117
Congo, 29
Congo Nile Trail, 11, 25, 113
Count Von Goetzen, 58

credit cards, 132, 137,

D

Democratic Republic of the Congo, 28
Dian Fossey, 35
Dian Fossey Gorilla Fund International, 143
Dismas Nsengiyaremye, 65
Dodoma, 78
DRC. *See* Democratic Republic of Congo
Durban, 159

E

East Africa, 1, 3, 6, 63, 74, 104, 112, 116, 144, 160, 229

East Africa
Company, 74
England, 7, 81,
142
Entebbe, 3, 15,
25, 40, 79, 82,
84, 97, 108,
109, 129
Entebbe Botanical
Gardens, 101
Equator, 19, 61,
94, 166
Equatorial
Guinea, 29

F

Faustin
Twagiramungu
a, 69
France, 64, 65, 81,
84, 85, 142

G

Gabon, 29

General Juvenal
Habyarimana,
64
Germany, 81
Godfrey Binaisa,
85
Gold, 157, 159
gorilla permit, 38,
39
gorilla safari, 25,
37, 38, 39, 40,
110, 126, 145,
223
gorillas, 201
*Gorillas in the
Mist*, 36

H

Health, 130
Henry Stanley, 74
Hutu, 58, 60, 63,
64, 66, 67, 87,
160

I

Idi Amin, 76, 83, 84, 85
inoculations. *See* vaccinations
iSafari, 207

J

Jinga, 97, 98
Jinji, 82
Johannesburg, 159
John Hanning Speke, 81
Joseph Kony, 86

K

Kampala, 3, 10, 13, 19, 78, 94, 98, 109, 129, 153, 154
Karisimbi Volcano, 71
Kasabi Tombs, 99
Kazinga Channel, 105

Kenya, 78, 101, 142, 157
Kibale Forest, 91
Kibale National Park, 99
Kidepo Valley National Park, 99
Kigali, 3, 10, 16, 61, 66, 67, 68, 69, 71, 73, 111, 113, 114, 117, 129, 155
Kigali Genocide Memorial, 114
Kinyarwanda, 119
KwaZulu-Natal, 197

L

Lake Kivu, 25, 68, 69
Lake Mburo National Park, 100
Lake Victoria, 10, 19, 78, 81, 83,

94, 97, 98, 101,
104, 107, 108,
110, 157
languages, 118
lemurs, 201
Lesotho, 124
Lord's Resistance
Army, 86, 87
lowland gorilla, 9,
28
LRA. *See* Lord's
Resistance
Army
Lubiri Palace, 99

M

Madagascar, 12,
201
malaria, 131
medications, 138
Mgahinga Gorilla
National Park,
101
Milton Obote, 83,
85
Money, 131
mountain gorilla,
28, 157
Murchison Falls
National Park,
11, 103, 104,
108
Mwami
Tutsi King, 58,
63

N

Nairobi, 78, 142
National Animal
of South Africa,
27
National flag of
South Africa,
16
National
Resistance
Army, 77, 85
Ngamba Island
Chimpanzee
Sanctuary, 104

Nile River, 97, 98, 103
Northern Hemisphere, 21
Nyungwe Forest National Park, 114, 118

O

Operation Turquoise, 68

P

Pack. See What To Pack
PARMEHUTU Hutu Emancipation Movement, 63
passport, 122, 128
Pearl of Africa, 8, 79, 82
Population, 14
President Clinton, 68
Pretoria, 159
Priceline., 216
public holidays, 149

Q

Queen Elizabeth National Park, 3, 11, 94, 105, 180

R

rainy season, 200
Republic of Rwanda. *See* Rwanda
Rift Valley, 103, 204
Rwanda, 1, 3, 4, 7, 12, 14, 16, 18, 19, 20, 21, 24, 25, 26, 27, 28, 36, 38, 39, 51, 56, 58, 60, 62, 63, 64, 65, 66, 68, 69, 70, 71, 78, 87, 89, 91, 102, 111,

112, 114, 115, 119, 122, 125, 126, 144, 145, 149, 151, 152, 155, 156, 157, 158, 160, 201, 229
Rwanda Parliament, 61
Rwanda Tourism Board, 145
Rwandan Patriotic Front, 65, 66, 67
Rwenzori Mountains, 106

S

safari, 148
Safari, 3, 120
Safety, 128
Sanctuary Gorilla Forest Camp, 55
Seasons of South Africa, 22
Semuliki National Park, 106
Smart Traveler Enrollment Program, 123
Snake Park, 109
Southern Hemisphere, 21, 61
Ssese Islands Hidden Islands, 11, 107
STA Travel, 215
Sudan, 78, 87
Sun City, 206
Surfing, 27
Swahili, 119

T

Tanzania, 64, 77, 85, 101, 157, 202

Technical Military Assistance Agreement, 64
Theodore Sindikubwabo, 67
tip. *See* Tipping
Tipping, 121
Tito Okello, 85
travel agents, 144
Travel Documents, 122
Travel Insurance, 124
Travel Warnings, 124
travelers cheques, 131
TSA, 140
Tutsi, 58, 60, 63, 64, 67, 114, 150, 160

U

U.S. Embassy, 123
UDPF. *See* Ugandan Peoples Defense Force
Uganda, 1, 3, 4, 7, 12, 13, 14, 15, 17, 18, 19, 20, 21, 22, 24, 25, 27, 28, 38, 39, 40, 51, 55, 64, 65, 67, 74, 81, 82, 83, 84, 85, 86, 87, 88, 89, 90, 91, 94, 95, 98, 99, 100, 101, 102, 104, 108, 116, 122, 125, 126, 144, 145, 150, 151, 153, 154, 155, 156, 157, 158, 159, 161, 194, 201, 229
Uganda Museum, 99
Uganda Tourism Board, 145

Ugandan Peoples Defense Force, 86
Umuganda, 62
UN. *See* United Nations
Unique Experiences, 25
United Nations, 66, 83

V

Vaccinations, 125
Victoria Mall, 108
Virunga Mountains, 3, 71, 101, 116
visa (tourist), 122
Volcanoes National Park, 3, 11, 52, 56, 115

W

water, 126
weather, 20
wildlife, 7, 120, 148
Winston Churchill, 82
World Bank, 69

Y

yellow fever certificate, 125
Yoweri Museveni, 85, 86
Yusufu Lule, 85

Z

Zaire, 29, 68, 69, 87
Ziwa Rhino Sanctuary, 108

Printed by Amazon Italia Logistica S.r.l.
Torrazza Piemonte (TO), Italy